DIVIDED BY HISTORY

ROOTS OF SUDANESE CONFLICT

Peter Dixon

Cloudshill Press
Cheltenham and London, United Kingdom

Copyright © 2019 by Peter Dixon.

Every reasonable effort has been taken to trace copyright holders of material reproduced in this book, but if any have been inadvertently overlooked the Publisher would be glad to hear from them.

Cover image: Anglo-Egyptian Sudanese camel soldier, photograph by Frank G Carpenter (1855-1924). US Library of Congress Prints and Photographs Division, Washington DC Reference LC-USZC2-6349.

Copyright details for images are provided in the List of Images, whose content is deemed to be part of this copyright page.

Peter Dixon asserts his moral right to be identified as the author of this book.

All rights reserved. No part of this publication may be reproduced, distributed or transmitted in any form or by any means, electronic or mechanical, including photocopying, recording or by any information storage and retrieval system, without prior written permission of the Publisher.

Published by Cloudshill Press LLP

Registered Office: 27 Old Gloucester Street, London WC1N 3AX United Kingdom

All enquiries to **info@cloudshillpress.com**

Book Layout ©2015 BookDesignTemplates.com

Ordering Information:

Quantity sales: special discounts are available on quantity purchases by corporations, associations and others. For details, contact the publisher at info@cloudshillpress.com.

Divided by History / Peter Dixon. -- 1st ed.

ISBNs	Paper	978-0-9935080-9-7
	Ebook	978-1-9160273-0-5

*For the people of Sudan and South Sudan,
who deserve better*

The further backward you look, the further forward you can see.

—Winston Churchill

Contents

Then affects now 1
Egypt and Kush 9
The Turks and the Mahdi 19
The Condominium 47
War and Peace 63
Chronology 75
Research Sources and Further Reading 77
Acknowledgements 81
List of Images 83
About the Author 85
Bibliography 87
Index 91
Notes 95

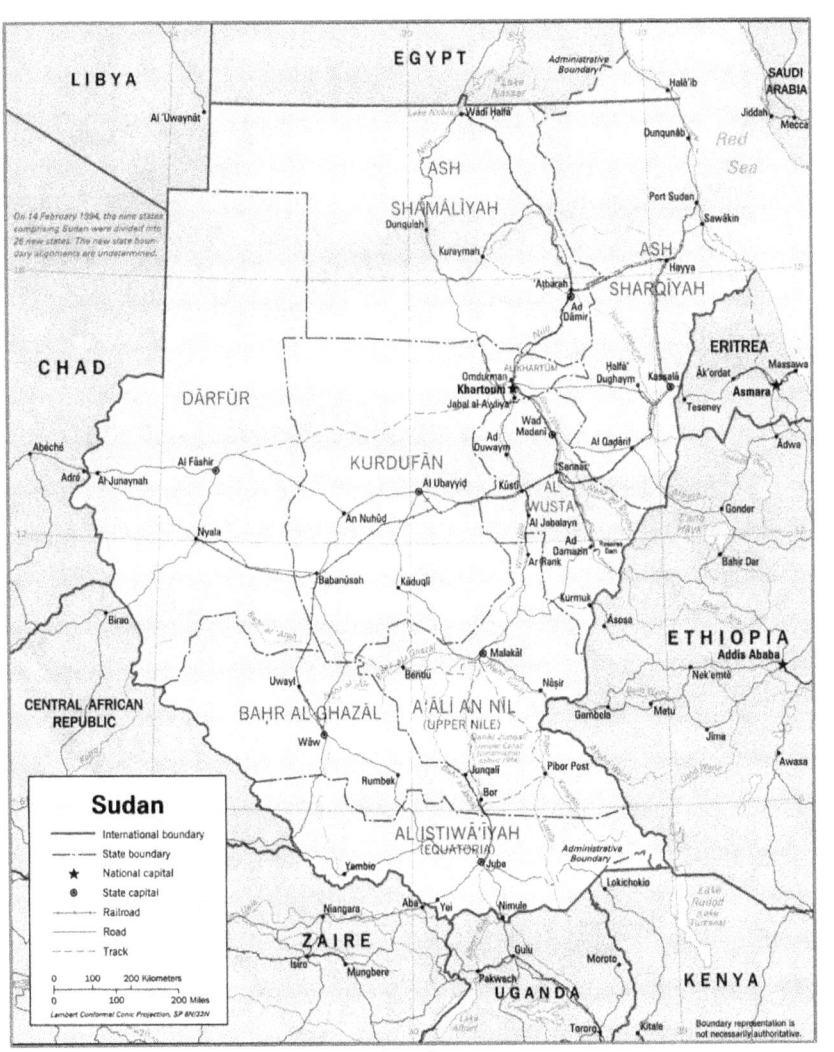

Sudan political map, 1994

CHAPTER ONE

Then affects now

Juba

It is a Sunday morning in the spring of 2009. I sit in the back row of All Saints' Cathedral in Juba, the capital of South Sudan. I watch in fascination as a procession of children sways up the central aisle of the church in time with their well-rehearsed song. An eleven-year-old boy leads the procession and the singing. A six-year-old at the tail of the procession looks a little nonplussed, but overall they are a happy sight. They reach the altar, line up and turn to face the congregation. The music – sung in that enchanting shrill, piercing style peculiar to Africa – gives way to a joyful ululation from the 500 worshippers. All applaud. Such a line used to be called a 'crocodile' when my children were at school. It seems apt, a couple of miles from the White Nile.

The church service was a celebration of peace, but most of these children were born into war. Even their parents had seen little else. Civil war had raged for all but eleven of the years since Sudan gained its independence in 1956.

Fast-forward two years to 9th July 2011. Jubilant men, women and children crowd the streets of Juba to celebrate the independence of the new state of South Sudan. For them, this day is the culmination of decades of struggle to gain their freedom. Around the world, many sympathise with the well-publicised plight of the southern Sudanese people. They enthusiastically greet the creation of the 193rd member state of the United Nations. Some Sudanese to the north, though, see the day as the end of seventy-eight months that were meant to 'make unity attractive'.

The starting pistol for that 6-month Pre-Interim Period and 6-year Interim Period - seventy-eight months in all - was the so-called Comprehensive Peace Agreement. The CPA was signed on 9th January 2005 by the two main combatants: the Government of Sudan and the Sudan People's Liberation Movement/Army, the SPLM/A. It is commonly known as the Naivasha Agreement, after the Kenyan resort where negotiators agreed most of its complex components. It brought the second of two Sudanese civil wars to an end.

The various protocols covered a wide spectrum of issues: transition to democratic governance, security arrangements, power-sharing and wealth-sharing. The agreement also included documents covering the regional disputes in areas close to the north-south border: the Abyei area and Southern Kordofan and Blue Nile States. Richer countries and international organisations promised vast sums of development aid: a 'peace dividend' for a land and people devastated by bloody civil war.

Yet the initial euphoria soon dissipated. The Interim Period passed relatively peacefully, but the CPA had left many issues unresolved. The civil war that had just ended was not simply a two-sided conflict, to be solved by negotiations between two 'players'. Instead, it was a complex web of interconnected conflicts, rooted in ethnic and religious identity, economic inequality and competition for resources and power.

Perhaps the divisive outcome of the waiting period could have been foreseen years earlier. Suffice it to say that many factors prevented the protagonists from using the 'breathing space' to settle the outstanding issues and create a democratic New Sudan. In a referendum in January 2011, almost 99% of the southern Sudanese people voted for independence from Sudan. Six months later, it became fact.

But even that momentous decision did not bring peace. In July 2016, that same cathedral provided sanctuary for 1,000 people fleeing gun battles in the streets of Juba. Soldiers loyal to the President, Salva Kiir, fought armed men supporting his Vice President, Riek Machar. This was just one violent episode of many, in a struggle between ethnic groups for power in the new state.

Modern South Sudan

The peace process that culminated in southern Sudanese secession was a partial success. Yet almost continuous hostility between Sudan and South Sudan has blighted the years since southern independence. Inter-ethnic violence within both countries has not helped. Armed conflict has continued, and the complexities of Sudanese conflict are by no means resolved.

Deep Roots

The Comprehensive Peace Agreement signed on 9th January 2005 resulted from years of mediated negotiations. It brought to an end the long-running civil war between the North and South of Sudan. Several writers have described the peace process that led to the signature of the agreement. I will cover the process only briefly in a later chapter. Enough comprehensive histories of Sudan exist, so I do not intend adding to their number. Rather, I focus on outside intervention, as important in the past as it is today. I tell the stories of some of the outsiders who have intervened over the centuries in what is now Sudan and South Sudan. In doing so, I aim to dig out the deep historical and cultural roots of recent Sudanese conflicts hidden in those stories. Robert Collins suggested in 2008 that 'any understanding of Sudan today is to be found in the events of the last 200 years'.[1] That may be true. As Collins suggests, though, the Egyptian, Ottoman Turkish, Arab and British cultures were successively imposed on a country that was already very large, geographically and climatically diverse, and ethnically divided.

Sudan is big. Today's Sudan and South Sudan together cover an area of 2.5 million square kilometres. Depending on where you live, you may prefer to see it as one-third the size of Australia, or a quarter of the area of the United States. Or you could just imagine that you could fit France into it five times over.

Geographically, the key feature of Sudan is of course the mighty River Nile, which has been one of the most significant resources for millennia. It is also a source of conflict. The Nile dominates: Winston Churchill called it 'the life of the lands through which it flows' and 'the great melody that recurs throughout the whole opera'.[2] The Nile originates as the Blue Nile in the Ethiopian Plateau and the White Nile in the Equatorial Lakes shared by Uganda, Kenya and Tanzania. After dropping from the Lakes, the White Nile crosses a large area of marshland known as the Sudd and then flows around the Eastern edge of the Nuba Mountains. After passing either side of the fertile *gezira* plain, the Blue and White Niles converge. Stand on the bridge connecting Khartoum and Omdurman and you can see the different colours of the water flowing in from the two rivers.

Sudan's geography and climate encompass extremes. We can easily imagine the difference between the rich soils close to the River Nile and the arid desert plains further away. But we may not be aware of the fertile uplands around the Jebel Marra in Darfur, which rises to over 3,000 metres (10,000 feet). Or the range of hills along the Red Sea coast rising to heights of up to 2,000 metres (6,000 feet). Or the Nuba mountains rising 1,000 metres (3,000 feet) or so from the surrounding plain in South Kordofan. Or the tangle of channels, lakes and swamp that cover about 30,000 square kilometres (12,000 square miles) in the impenetrable Sudd. The oppressive heat of the parched desert contrasts with winter temperatures falling close to freezing. Annual rainfall varies from less than 10 centimetres to over a metre (3 inches to 3 feet). I have experienced the *haboob* sandstorms that hit Khartoum from time to time, obscuring the sun and turning day into night.

Importantly for the purposes of this book, the cultures of the Sudanese people are no less diverse.

Verdant garden in Darfur, 2008

Who are the Sudanese?

If you dig deep enough, all countries are complex in their ethnic mix. But Sudan, before it was divided into two states, was among the most complex and diverse; the 'two Sudans' remain so today. The impression we gain from television and newspapers is of a simple division into northern Muslim 'Arabs' and southern Christian or animist 'Africans'. Yet this does not nearly do justice to the estimated 600 ethnic and linguistic groups.

Amir Idris suggests that this two-part picture of Sudanese identity results from the historical construction of an 'orientalist' North and a 'prehistoric' South, reinforced by the sustained practice of slavery.[3] We will look into this further as the story develops. Yet, without giving such a false impression, simplifying the ethnic composition of the Sudanese people can still help our understanding.

Most of the Arab Muslims of the North can be roughly divided into two groups: settled 'Arabised Nubians' who live close to the Nile - the right term is 'riverain' - and nomadic or semi-nomadic *juhayna* whose ancestors came from southern Arabia via Upper Egypt. Additional, non-Arab groups of Muslims include the Beja of Eastern Sudan and the Western Sudanese Masali, Zaghawa and Fur. The name Darfur, well-known internationally, literally means 'the land of the Fur'. A further proudly distinct group is the Nuba, a linguistically and culturally complex collection of ethnic communities formerly living in isolation in the Nuba Mountains.

Non-Muslim groups primarily inhabit the South, relatively settled but not clustered as close to the Nile as in the drier North. Water for agriculture is more widely available. Of approximately sixty southern tribal groups, the Dinka and Nuer are today the two most powerful. Deep-rooted oral traditions relate when different groups migrated into the area, where they came from, and whom they displaced in the often-violent process. Memories of these clashes can fuel conflict even today. The number of languages in use reflects the ethnic diversity. But local forms of Arabic are widespread, and English is widely spoken among educated people in the South.

For centuries, inter-marriage, trade and migration have blurred the racial, religious and geographic dividing lines in Sudan. Nevertheless, the north-south 'fault line', which has contributed to violent conflict, cannot be denied. It is symbolised by one of the major stumbling blocks to achieving a political settlement faced by the Naivasha mediators: Khartoum's commitment to *shari'a* law and the SPLM's secularist agenda.

Ancient and Modern

The themes of diversity, ethnic conflict and imperialism have existed in Sudan for thousands of years. I aim in this book to travel back in time to see how stories of long ago affect current events. In particular, we will see how outside influences have shaped the history of Sudan and formed the seedbed from which violent conflict has grown. This brief look at the historical background of a controversial current situation may be helpful to readers who like to explore what lies behind newspaper headlines and television news reports.

In attempting this task, I am well aware of the ways in which historical facts and claims can be contested. 'Who writes the history?' is always an important question to ask. Gaining consensus on the past is a key element of reconciliation in divided societies. So I should make clear at the outset that I have no axe to grind. I write this book as the former Chief Executive of Concordis International, a British non-profit peace-building organisation.

Concordis spent over a decade impartially facilitating dialogue between and among the people of what were then parts of a single country. My colleagues and I provided a neutral space in which key individuals from all parts of Sudan - North, South, East and West - could work together on the issues that divided them. They sought common ground and found ways to overcome their differences. We worked alongside and in support of the negotiations to which the events of the brief history that follows were leading. I am no fan of the single-issue 'It's all about …' approach to the causes of conflict. As we examine Sudanese history in the following chapters, we discover the complexity that lies at the roots of the two civil wars, deep in the colonial, pre-colonial and even the ancient history of Sudan. The next chapter takes us back over 4,000 years to the Egyptian pharaohs.

CHAPTER TWO

Egypt and Kush

Journeys into Egypt's frontier lands

Around 2300 BC, a man named Harkhuf travelled from Egypt into the 'Southern Lands' we now know as Sudan. He was a successful leader of trading caravans. This was his third expedition into Nubia and beyond, each lasting eight or nine months and mounted on behalf of King Merenre of the Sixth Egyptian Dynasty. On his previous journeys, Harkhuf had brought back goods from Nubia that, according to his own account, had never reached Egypt before. He had opened up new areas to the south. Like nineteenth-century traders and explorers in America's 'wild west' frontier lands, he had made his fortune and reputation.

Just like the first two forays into the dangerous unknown, Harkhuf's third expedition had a small military escort. His donkeys carried Egyptian products as gifts and to barter: ointments, honey, woven clothing and fine pottery objects. He set out on the 'road of the oasis'. Travelling through 300 miles of mostly waterless desert, he searched for the ruler of Yam, a kingdom whose exact location is no longer known today. This ruler had headed off into the Libyan desert to the west on a military raid. Harkhuf followed him there and used all his diplomatic skills to 'pacify' him, persuading him to trade rather than make war.

Harkhuf sent a message back to King Merenre, informing him that he had made a good trade with Yam. He headed back to the Nile, reaching it at Tushka, just north of Wadi Halfa. To protect his 300 donkeys, an escort of Yam tribesmen travelled back with him. The beasts carried incense, ebony, special oil for worship, choice grains, leopard skins and ivory. On the way, Harkhuf passed through the regions of Irthet, Sethu, and Wawat, where the local chiefs had given him trouble in the past. But when they saw the strength of the company of Yam fighters with him, they contributed oxen and goats to his 'haul'. They conducted him safely through a secret path to the Nile, where boats sent by the king met him and brought him safely home.

Harkhuf from tomb at Qubbet el-Hawa

Harkhuf's reputation grew even stronger and King Merenre's young successor, Pepy II, sent him on further journeys to the south. On one, he brought back a pygmy as a curiosity for the king. In reply to Harkhuf's letter announcing this gift, King Pepy urged caution. 'Take care that the pygmy does not fall into the river,' he wrote, 'or meet with any other accident on the journey down to Memphis'.[4]

The journeys of Harkhuf were just a few among many that took place before and after his time. Not all were as peaceful. The same King Pepy II sent expedition leader Pepynekht with a large force to devastate Irthet, Sethu, and Wawat. Pepynekht slaughtered many of the local people, including children of the chief and senior members of his court, and brought away a great number of captives.

Egyptian influence over the area kept open the routes for caravans bringing exotic goods from Eastern and Central Africa. The trading routes were essential to the income of successive pharaohs, so the areas through which caravans passed had to be subdued. Defensive forts were built at key locations. Once again, the parallel with the American West of the nineteenth century is clear.

The Sudanese economy has had an extractive character for thousands of years. Experts in violent conflict often talk about 'the curse of riches'. Resources that ought to be of benefit to the people end up being fought over or seized by outsiders. In Sudan, early traders dealt in gold, ivory, and slaves. By the twentieth century, this trade had been superseded by revenues from agriculture and the oil that lay in abundance beneath the surface. But rich resources continued to fuel conflict.

Nubian Viceroys

Seen from ancient Egypt, the untamed 'Southern Lands' were a vast area that more or less encompassed what we now know as Sudan and South Sudan. Even though the ancient Egyptians called the inhabitants 'wretched', they were still keen to control the area to the south. They did not see the area's resources as particularly enticing. But at the very least they needed safe passage along the trade routes that ran between Egypt and Central Africa. Along these caravan roads passed the gold, slaves and exotic goods that reinforced the power of the pharaohs.

The greatest challenge to Egyptian dominance of the lands to their south was the ancient kingdom of Kush, centred on Kerma in the northern part of modern Sudan. Over the centuries, Kush's star fell and rose as the power of the Egyptian civilisation waxed and waned. By 2000 BC, Kush was challenging Egyptian dominance of Nubia. However, a resurgent Egypt, at the height of its power in the Eighteenth Dynasty, brought this early period of Kush prominence to an end in about 1500 BC.

For the next five centuries, Egypt administered Nubia as a colony under a series of viceroys, mostly appointed for life. The first was Thury, appointed by the pharaoh Amenhotep I as 'king's son, Governor of the Southern Lands'. He was still in post when Thutmose I succeeded Amenhotep, but Nubia was by no means pacified. King Thutmose led an army to the south in about 1538 BC, ordering Thury to have a canal dug out; he had found it choked with stones. Water transport was a key to military mobility. Thutmose succeeded in defeating the Kushites:

> His Majesty came downstream, all countries in his grasp, with the wretched Nubian chief hanging head downwards on the prow of the royal barge, and landed at Thebes.[5]

The forts and key trading posts in the Southern Lands were filled with Egyptian merchants, soldiers, priests and officials, with their families. Gradually, the area became Egyptianised. Each viceroy only ruled over the northern part of Sudan, but his duties extended to political and commercial relations with the tribal leaders beyond his borders. The main purpose was to collect as much wealth as possible for the pharaoh as tribute: slaves, cattle, gum arabic, hides, hardwood, ebony, ivory, ostrich eggs, ostrich feathers and especially gold.

The most famous pharaoh today is probably Tutankhamun, whose viceroy in Nubia was the seventh to serve there, a nobleman by the name of Huwy. Huwy's tomb, near Thebes, shows how he was summoned into the presence of the king to be appointed as viceroy. The Overseer of the Treasury says to him: 'This is the seal from the pharaoh, who assigns to you the territory from El-Kah to Napata'. Another official hands the seal to Huwy, saying: 'Take the seal, O King's Son of Kush'. Other scenes in the carving show Huwy's ship departing for Napata, and shiploads of booty being delivered to Thebes.[6]

Nothing lasts forever, though, and Egyptian political influence over Nubia declined from about 1100 BC. The Kushite viceroys progressively exerted their autonomy. The kingdom of Kush effectively became independent again and gradually increased in strength. Even though Egyptian cultural influence remained strong, the tables were turned.

The leaders of Kush built pyramids, called themselves pharaohs and practised Egyptian forms of worship. Their economic and military power continued to increase. Initially conquering the Upper Nile region as far as Luxor, they eventually took control of a weakened Egypt as far as the Mediterranean Sea. They became Egypt's 25th Dynasty: the 'Black Pharaohs'. But this Kushite or Nubian dynasty in Egypt lasted only a century. Assyrian invaders defeated the Kushites and drove them back to Nubia during the period 671 to 654 BC.

A story from just a few decades after the Kushite retreat shows us that dynasties like the Kushites did not live in isolation from others. International travel and the expatriate life are not only recent features of globalisation. The Biblical book of Jeremiah tells how Ebed-Melek, a Kushite expatriate working for King Zedekiah in Jerusalem, saved Jeremiah's life. Powerful officials had put the troublesome prophet into a water cistern that contained only deep mud, and left him to die. The compassionate Kushite Ebed-Melek heard of this and called on the king to let him save Jeremiah. He rushed to the cistern with ropes, old rags for Jeremiah to put under his arms as padding, and thirty men for protection. They pulled the prophet out of the muddy cistern and he lived on, to prophesy further.[7]

Kush continued as an independent kingdom in Northern Sudan until its decline by AD 350. From the middle of the sixth century AD, two Christian kingdoms, Nobadia and Alwah, became established, with strong Coptic and Byzantine Greek influence.

The Christian Kingdoms and the Spread of Islam

We may sometimes imagine that women in powerful leadership positions are a modern phenomenon. Not so. Think of Cleopatra. Think of Eleanor of Aquitaine. These women represented exceptions to the general rule: that men rule. One such exceptional woman was Theodora, from AD 527 to 548 Empress of the Byzantine Empire, which ruled much of the Middle East from its capital at today's Istanbul.

Empress Theodora

Theodora married Emperor Justinian I after an early life as a disreputable actress and courtesan. She probably played as great a role in the politics of Byzantium as did her husband the Emperor. She became a devotee of the heretical Monophysite[8] sect of Christianity during her time in Alexandria. Both she and the more orthodox Justinian sent preachers and missionaries to Nubia. Theodora's missionaries gained greater popularity than those sent by the Emperor. Starting with Nobadia, the rulers of several independent kingdoms converted to one or other form of Christianity. As was the custom, they mostly took their followers with them.

However, Nubia had felt Christian influence long before this. The eighth chapter of the Acts of the Apostles describes how Philip baptised an Ethiopian eunuch on the way from Jerusalem to Gaza. The Ethiopia of the time covered a much greater area than that we see on today's maps and, according to legend, this man later became Patriarch of Nubia. The legend stands on shaky ground, but visits by Coptic monks from Egypt in the fourth century are better substantiated.

Whatever their origins, Nobadia and Alwah (or Alodia) were the most prominent of several Christian kingdoms that arose from the sixth century onwards. Nobadia, which incorporated the kingdom of Makuria, had its capital at Old Dongola (Dunqulah) and dominated the northern part of today's Sudan. Numerous small Byzantine churches were built. A few have been excavated.

Ruins of Church of the Granite Columns, Old Dongola

The southern kingdom of Alwah is more mysterious, even though it existed to a later date and was probably more powerful than Nobadia. Its capital at Soba, on the banks of the Blue Nile, was a substantial town. The tenth-century Egyptian diplomat and traveller Ibn Selim el-Aswani reported that it contained fine buildings, extensive dwellings and gardens, monasteries and churches full of gold.[9]

By the seventh century, both kingdoms were already under increasing threat from Muslim culture and military invaders. At first, Nobadia in the north could halt any advance from Egypt, and was able to make trade agreements: Egyptian fabrics and grain for African slaves. Over the centuries the pressure increased, though, and Islam became the dominant religion. The church at Dongola had become a mosque by AD 1317 and the Christians of Nobadia were finally defeated in a battle in AD 1323.

Further south, the threat to the kingdom of Alwah developed later. Especially after the defeat of Nobadia, the Christians of Alwah became more isolated and their culture gradually declined. They were an easy target for the rapidly expanding Funj Sultanate, recent converts to Islam, whose capital was at Sennar, also on the Blue Nile. The Funj destroyed Alwah's capital, Soba, in the early sixteenth century.

It is easy to cite specific battles and approximate dates when the Christian kingdoms were militarily defeated. However, these events took place alongside a more subtle and gradual change. Arab travellers and traders, from across the Red Sea to the east, and Egyptians from the north brought pottery, glass objects and textiles such as Fatimid silk.

They also brought their culture and religion with them. The 'Christian' city of Suba, for example, included Muslim merchants' quarters.

So the Christian religion succumbed gradually to the inexorable challenge of a new cultural and religious force, Islam. Religious difference would prove one of the powerful causes of violence in the coming centuries and is cited by many as the prime cause of the modern north-south civil wars. But that is too simple a view.

The Funj and Darfur

As Islamic scholars from Arabia founded mosques and Koranic schools, the cultural influence of Islam gradually spread across Sudan. Culture incorporates language. The use of Arabic became widespread in religion, education and administration. But groups like the Beja of eastern Sudan, the Shilluk of central Sudan and the Fur in the West still spoke indigenous languages in a domestic setting. Cultural developments took place ahead of major political and military influx by Islamic leaders. Yet this did come.

The first Islamic state of any size in the area was the Funj dynasty. By the end of the seventeenth century, it had annihilated the Christian state of Alwah, repulsed advances by the Shilluk kingdom and extended its control of southern Nubia. From the north, Ottoman forces who had conquered Egypt in AD 1517 advanced beyond the third cataract on the River Nile and prevented any further northward expansion by the Funj.

To the west, meanwhile, an independent Muslim sultanate dominated by the Fur people was being established. The town of Al-Fashir, in what is now northern Darfur, eventually became its capital. Suleiman Solon ('Suleiman the Red"), founder of the Keira dynasty, is considered to have laid the foundations of the sultanate of Darfur in AD 1637. At its height in the eighteenth century, it controlled territory stretching to the banks of the White Nile. Al-Fashir had long been a halting place for caravans plying the trade routes between Egypt and West Africa, but was established as the dynasty's capital in 1790. Darfur's traditional independence from the rest of Sudan lies close to the heart of the modern Darfur crisis that blighted attempts to settle the second north-south civil war.

The Impact of Ancient History

The picture emerges of a region dominated for long periods of ancient history by the highly developed Egyptian civilisation. However, the area contained proud, independent kingdoms that could sometimes challenge

Egypt and, in the case of the Kush kingdom during the eighth century BC, conquer it. Kush was pushed back to its Nubian homeland but survived there until the fourth century AD. Two Christian kingdoms - Nobadia and Alwah - filled the vacuum Kush left behind. They dominated Nubia for a further thousand years. However, Islamic culture seeped into Nubia and eventually led to the collapse of the Christian kingdoms. In the north, the Ottomans took their place. In southern Nubia, it was the Funj dynasty that dominated.

Things were different in the area further south, including the territory of the modern state of South Sudan. Not least because of the barrier formed by the swampy, mosquito-ridden Sudd, invasion from the north was hardly feasible. Ancient oral traditions tell the story of tribal groups - predominantly the Dinka and Nuer - migrating into the area in search of pasture. Indigenous groups like the Shilluk defended the land on which they depended for subsistence. Disputes were often resolved with violence, but sometimes the chiefs achieved peaceful solutions, often involving inter-marriage and assimilation. Competition between pastoralists and more settled farmers remains a key element of civil war in South Sudan and Sudan today, almost a millennium later.

The records also show that the southern and other peripheral regions were used as staging areas for the well-organised and profitable exploitation of resources from deeper into Africa. Then as now, the economy was extractive. The 'goods' extracted included slaves, but also gold, ivory, ebony, cattle, hides and ostrich feathers. The foundations were being laid for treating central Sudan differently from the peripheral areas, particularly the South.

CHAPTER THREE

The Turks and the Mahdi

Muhammad Ali Pasha

What has the son of an Albanian merchant, from a small town in what is now northern Greece, to do with the causes of conflict in Sudan? For one thing, he ruled Nubia for much of the nineteenth century, and that with an iron fist. He contributed to the extractive, colonialist treatment of Sudan.

Muhammad Ali Pasha has been called the founder of modern Egypt. He came from relatively humble origins but eventually ruled all of Egypt and Sudan, not to mention other parts of the Middle East. He grew up in the Macedonian town of Kavala, where his merchant father married into a prominent local family. The merchant died early, and the boy was taken in by his influential uncle. The uncle put Muhammad to work in the local administration, eventually appointing him as town tax collector.

In 1801, international politics intervened. By then, French troops were occupying Egypt. Three years earlier, Emperor Napoleon Bonaparte had defeated the Mamluks, warriors who had risen from the ranks of slave-soldiers to occupy Egypt for half a millennium. The brief French occupation had a significant influence on Egypt's culture and archaeology, but Napoleon withdrew after just three years and left a military and political vacuum. Egypt was ripe for re-occupation.

Muhammad Ali Pasha, by Auguste Couder, 1840

An Ottoman mercenary force was assembled for that purpose, and the town of Kavala raised a volunteer contingent to join it. Thanks to the influence of his uncle, Muhammad Ali became its second in command. On landing in Egypt, the Ottomans fought the weakened Mamluk forces and continued to vie with them for power.

Muhammad Ali was more skilful politician than soldier. For the next few years he worked with both sides, forging alliances and gaining popular support. He ruthlessly neutralised the Mamluk threat in 1811, by inviting the Mamluk leaders to a celebration in Cairo and having them surrounded and killed. His army could then defeat the decapitated Mamluk forces throughout Egypt. Many of the Mamluks scattered into Sudan and further afield.

Once he had established control, Muhammad Ali set about transforming Egypt. He built roads and canals. He taxed property-owners and took control of the economy. He developed the production of cotton for export, weapons for the army and ships for the navy. Meanwhile, he initiated a new legal structure, reformed education and introduced European-style training for the government and military. Security was his main concern, and he built up a conscript army that turned Egypt into a major regional power. Although as Viceroy he was in theory subordinate to the Sultan in Constantinople (Istanbul), he acted independently and harboured ambitions to found a dynasty that would rival the declining Ottoman Empire. He called himself the 'Khedive' of Egypt.

Equipped with modernised armed forces and having consolidated his control of Lower Egypt, Muhammad Ali was ambitious to gain territory, ostensibly on behalf of the Ottoman Sultan. His military campaigns to challenge Saudi control of Arabia and the holy cities of Medina and Mecca were eventually successful, leaving him free to turn his attention to Sudan. In 1820, he sent his third son, Ismail, at the head of an army of about 5,000 men to subdue the disorganised Sudanese tribes.

The army was a hotchpotch of conscripts and mercenaries of various nationalities: from Turkey, Albania, the Egyptian desert, the Maghreb and even the USA. In command of the artillery was George Bethune English, an American adventurer born in Cambridge, Massachusetts. After a time in the American West, English had received a commission in the United States Marine Corps and was sent to the Mediterranean. During a visit to Egypt, he resigned his commission and converted to Islam. He had studied law and theology at Harvard but came to doubt the Christian faith.

George English was a willing volunteer in Ismail's army. In his view, 'Egypt, once the home of discord and the headquarters of anarchy, under [Viceroy Muhammad Ali's] administration has long enjoyed peace and prosperity, and is yearly progressing in wealth and improvement'. However, he claimed,

> For several years past the inland commerce of this favored land had suffered great interruptions from the confusion and discord to which the

countries on the Upper Nile have been a prey ... The civil wars ... had occasioned an almost entire cessation of a commerce, from which Egypt had derived great advantages. His Highness the Viceroy, in consequence, determined, as the most effectual means of putting an end to these disorders, to subject those countries to his dominion.[10]

Ismail's main mission in conquering the territory was to procure a supply of slaves for the army. The main resistance came from the Shaigiya tribe of the Merowe area, who were trained to be warriors from boyhood. According to Swiss traveller Johann Ludwig (a.k.a. John Lewis) Burckhardt:

> These different people are continually at war with each other, and their youth make plundering excursions as far as Darfour, to the west, and Wady Halfa, to the north. They all fight on horseback, in coats of mail ... Firearms are not common among them, their only weapons being a lance, target [a small round shield], and sabre; they throw the lance to a great distance with much dexterity, and always carry four or five lances in the left hand, when charging an enemy. They are all mounted on Dóngola stallions and are famous for their horsemanship.[11]

Inevitably, the superior weaponry and organisation of Muhammad Ali's troops prevailed. He incorporated the Shaigiya into his army, together with slaves captured from southern and eastern Sudan, forming the 'Jihadiya' regiment. (In the twentieth century civil wars, the Khartoum regime similarly co-opted some southern fighters.) The remnants of the Funj dynasty at Sennar surrendered in June 1821.

The turkiya

The invasion of Sudan in 1820-21 by Muhammad Ali, who had by now ruled Egypt on behalf of the Ottoman Sultan for a decade, led to six decades of rule and economic exploitation by the 'Egyptians'. Sudanese know the period as the *turkiya,* but both names are misnomers: the occupiers were neither Egyptian nor Turkish. The elites who ruled Egypt and eventually Sudan spoke the Turkish language but came from various countries.

These 'Egyptians' controlled and developed the areas of northern

Sudan close to the Nile but not much farther afield. Darfur and the Nuba Mountains remained effectively unconquered. Economic and political inequality between the centre and the periphery of Sudan, one of the causes of the modern conflicts, was already developing. Even in the occupied territory, the invaders continued to experience resistance. The cruel regime was pitiless, taxation was punitive and Muhammad Ali's demand for slaves was unrelenting. Not surprisingly, the Sudanese mounted a rebellion. Harassed by pinprick attacks in Sennar, Ismail moved to the town of Shendi, where his unreasonable demands provoked an enraged reaction. Ja'aliyin tribesmen under Mek Nimr set fire to the encampment where Ismail was sleeping and massacred him and his companions.

News of the uprising encouraged rebellion elsewhere, and the Egyptians had to evacuate many garrisons. Like the French under Nazi occupation in the 1940s, though, the Sudanese reaped a whirlwind. The response was brutal and punitive, leaving a trail of destruction and death as order was restored. Resentment of the Egyptians, and of the Shaigiya who supported them in establishing their control of central Sudan, continued for decades.

Fighting rebels and suppressing insurrection are little help in encouraging trade. Such instability is not conducive to providing a steady supply of slaves for the military or the homes of the rich. After the occupiers had brutally suppressed the early, disunited attempts at insurrection, they developed a more cooperative approach with the northern Sudanese, reducing taxation and incorporating Sudanese tribal leaders in the administration.

The town of Khartoum, where the White and Blue Niles merged, had been founded in the early 1820s as a military base but gradually became a trading hub. Weak governance by the Turkish/Egyptian regime, especially after Muhammad Ali's death in 1849, allowed Arab and European traders to gain influence and to operate quite freely. Turkish was the official language in the early nineteenth century, but Arabic remained the *lingua franca* of northern Sudan.

Khartoum was relatively cosmopolitan and Europeanised. German/Russian explorer Wilhelm Junker described the city in 1889 as 'a curious patchwork society, Turkish officials, rich merchants who had made their money in the South by methods that nobody enquired into too closely'.[12]

By the nineteenth century, Islam had spread through most of northern Sudan but traditional, mostly animist, religion was widespread in the South. Turkish/Egyptian influence - if not control - extended from Khartoum as far as the Red Sea to the east and the Darfur boundary to the west, and southwards into modern South Sudan with a base at Fashoda. In the South, their control did not extend far outside their isolated posts.

These fortified settlements – the equivalent of US Cavalry forts in America's 'Wild West' - existed to support the European traders and to some extent the Catholic missionaries. Expeditions in 1839-41 had eventually broken through the previously impenetrable, mosquito-ridden swamps of the Sudd and discovered the more promising region beyond it. Here they found cultivated farmland and flourishing wildlife. Herds of elephants roamed freely. The traders could meet the growing European demand for ivory, initially by buying tusks from the local tribes, later by themselves hunting and killing elephants. But the most lucrative profits still came from the trade in humans.

Slave-trading was not new. Burckhardt estimated in 1819 that about 5,000 slaves a year were sold in the market at Shendy, most under the age of fifteen. About half of them were taken east to be sold in Arabia, most of the remainder north to Egypt.[13] The number sent north had exploded by the year 1860, to over 10,000. Outsiders saw southern Sudan as there to be subdued and exploited; attitudes to the uncivilised 'savages' were condescending and hostile, well before the period of Sudanese history we think of as colonial.

From the 1850s, pressure to suppress the slave trade increased, but progress was painfully slow. In 1869 the westernised Khedive of Turkish

Egypt, another Ismail who was the grandson of Muhammad Ali, 'subcontracted' the effort to Europeans. He appointed British explorer Sir Samuel Baker as Governor of the southern Sudanese district of Equatoria. The new Governor was to extend control southwards beyond Gondokoro (close to modern Juba) and put an end to the slave trade. Baker and his successor in 1873, Colonel Charles George Gordon, succeeded through armed raids on adjacent sheikdoms to open up the White Nile as far as the Lakes plateau, but the slave trade remained difficult to suppress, despite Gordon's zeal to do so. Although Gordon did not himself succumb to illness, several of the British officers he brought with him fell sick. Some did not survive.

Gordon was a slim, wiry officer of the Royal Engineers, with blue eyes, an intense gaze and a deep Christian faith. His confidence in God's providence often made him appear fearless in the face of danger. But vested interests in Khartoum undermined his anti-slavery efforts; 'I had a great deal of trouble with the Governor-General, who tried to put obstacles in my way', he wrote to a friend.[14]

His resources were limited - 300 men at Gondokoro and 200 in another post at Latuko - and, he reported, 'it is not safe ½-mile outside the posts'. The working conditions were hard, too. Gordon reported: 'I have been a good deal worn and I fear my temper is *very, very bad* but the people are trying and it is no use unless one is *feared*'. He tried to intercept slavers' convoys, but could not trust those working for him; 'my own Mudir [administrator] let 1,600 slaves pass for £E360 [Egyptian pounds]'.

As well as pacifying the tribes in Equatoria, he established posts along the river upstream and opened up navigation as far as Lake Victoria. The Khedive wanted him to go further and force a route from the lakes to the Indian Ocean, but he did not think he could 'plunge into the interior' and leave the field open for the Khartoum administration, which was already trying to thwart him.

'I am obliged to act towards the natives ... in a way that forces my conscience', wrote Gordon. He reluctantly mounted razzias to collect grain to feed his troops. In another parallel to the 'Wild West' of the United States, the suppression of the native people was an inevitable consequence of expansion into the frontier lands.

Gordon also had qualms about opening up the western branch of the Nile, for he feared that he would only 'open it for the misery of the natives'. Frustrated, he felt that as soon as he left his post there would be 'a fine trade up here in slaves' and 'the Khartoum Europeans are all in with it, in spite of their words'. He considered the heart of the slave trade to be in the province of Bahr el-Gazal.

After a brief leave in England, Gordon gained greater authority in 1877 to crush the slave trade, when the Khedive agreed to install him as Governor-General of the whole of Sudan. In this position, he was free to do battle against the powerful slave-trader Al-Zubayr Rahma Mansur, who had been appointed Governor of Bahr el-Ghazal, and his son Suleiman. Two years later, Gordon felt able to say: 'I consider that the slave trade is at an end', but this was over-optimistic. His military skills did not match the political challenge he faced, and orders were rarely carried out to the extent he imagined. He admitted that 'the putting down of the slave trade has not pleased everyone'.

Soon afterwards, Ismail abdicated from his position in Cairo as Khedive, having failed to resist the demands of the Europeans who controlled his finances. The exhausted Gordon resigned and travelled back to Europe. But 'Gordon of Khartoum' would soon return to the city, with fateful consequences.

The mahdiya

It may seem from the previous section that economic issues, and particularly the trade in slaves and ivory, were the driving force behind the domination of Sudan by the repressive Turco-Egyptian regime and the increasingly influential official British presence. There is something to be said for this view. But religious difference was relevant too.

The Khedive in Cairo had appointed Christian Europeans, like Baker and Gordon, to take over positions of authority in Sudan. This provoked resentment. Despite their orientalist attitudes, these men spoke little Arabic and had even less cultural empathy. Yet religious difference within Islam itself also reared its head. The orthodox Islam imposed from Egypt, along with its legal structures, had little in common with the Islam of rural Sudan. This was a more mystical *sufi* form of the religion, whose adherents would congregate around a charismatic and ascetic master. In 1881, one such leader posed an existential threat to the already weakened Turco-Egyptian regime.

Muhammad Ahmad bin 'Abdallah

Muhammad Ahmad bin 'Abdallah came from a family of humble boat-builders, but chose as a young man to study under *sufi* religious masters. He developed a reputation as a holy leader and powerful speaker, and attracted large numbers of followers. In June 1881, he announced that the prophets had appointed him in visions to be the Mahdi, the expected prophetic messenger. The Islamic leaders loyal to the Ottoman Sultan rejected his claim. But the number of his *sufi* followers (the *ansar*) grew rapidly. Their motivations were varied: certainly in some cases piety, but some were also defending their interest in the slave trade and others were driven by loyalty to their tribal leaders. The Mahdi's rebel followers overwhelmed several Turco-Egyptian garrisons and captured weapons.

The British were by now occupying Egypt, so a British officer, Lieutenant-General William Hicks ('Hicks Pasha') commanded the Egyptian force sent to re-assert authority over Sudan. The courageous Hicks advanced towards El-Obeid, his column surrounded by hostile tribes, plagued by desertions and unable to find supplies of water. Despite being armed with machine guns, the force was overwhelmed in November 1883 by the rebels: the 'Dervishes'. Hicks was killed. Other British-led forces had greater success, but eventually the rebels controlled a large area of northern Sudan and possessed large quantities of modern weapons. Only a few garrison towns and ports remained in British/Egyptian hands in December 1883. The Government in London decided to withdraw altogether. But soldiers and civilians in Sudan were in danger.

Meanwhile Charles Gordon was coming to the end of a sojourn in Palestine, where his evangelical Christian faith and cultural curiosity had led him to investigate an alternative site in Jerusalem for the crucifixion of Jesus.[15] Public pressure mounted for Prime Minister William Gladstone to send General Gordon, who was due to travel to the Congo, to Khartoum instead. He had achieved fame for his earlier military success in China and was seen as a Sudan expert. The London press called for 'Chinese Gordon' to be dispatched to Sudan. As the Pall Mall Gazette overstated,

> We cannot send a regiment to Khartoum, but we can send a man who on more than one occasion has proved himself more valuable in similar circumstances than an entire army.[16]

An expansionist, imperialist faction in London, encouraged by Queen Victoria, outmanoeuvred Gladstone. Gordon too became more vocally aggressive, his utterances gleefully reported in the London press. He arrived in Khartoum in February 1884, supposedly to manage the withdrawal. But his line of retreat northwards was blocked by the rebels and he had in any case decided to hold the city; he was more than ready to die. He petitioned a reluctant Government for reinforcements to open up the route north, while building up the defences of Khartoum. Meanwhile, the Mahdists mounted a siege of the city. Gordon, his confidence bolstered by his Christian faith, held out for almost a year and refused Muhammad Ahmad's calls on him to surrender. The Mahdi's last letter was allegedly smuggled into the city by a man dressed as a woman, because a previous messenger had been shot before he reached the walls. In it he wrote:

> We do not wish you to perish with those who are doomed to perish, because we have frequently heard good of you. ... For this reason we have repeatedly written to you urging you to return to your own country where your virtue will achieve the highest honour.[17]

The Mahdi's last letter to General Gordon

The feeling of national humiliation and indignation in Britain, as relief columns failed to break through and rescue Gordon's beleaguered garrison, almost brought Gladstone's government down. On the morning of 26th January 1885, the Mahdi's forces advanced on Khartoum and captured it after a battle lasting barely an hour. The events were portrayed with doubtful accuracy in a 1966 film, starring Charlton Heston as Gordon and Laurence Olivier as the Mahdi. Gordon was killed, despite the Mahdi's order that he should be spared, heard by an *ansar* eyewitness 'with my own ears'.[18]

Two days later, the first of the relief troops arrived. The late arrival was probably not as significant as it seemed; the Mahdists would probably have attacked earlier if necessary to pre-empt the arrival of reinforcements. Nevertheless, Gordon's death caused a sensation in Britain and elsewhere in Europe. The public saw Gordon as a hero and a martyr. Vengeance for his death was not far from the minds of the military. Gladstone took the blame for the disaster, but there was no prospect, for the time being, of the British re-taking Sudan.

Death of General Gordon at Khartoum, by J.L.G. Ferris, c. 1895

For the next thirteen years, Sudan effectively became a theocracy. The *sufi* believers who swore allegiance to the Mahdi and his successor Khalifa Abdullah al-Taaishi ruled over 'orthodox' Muslim and non-Muslim 'unbelievers'. But there was plenty of opposition from Fur, Masalit and Rizeigat groups in the West, from Ethiopia in the East and internally within Baqqara ranks. The *khalifa* struggled to keep control in a divided regime.

In southern Sudan, the Mahdists achieved even less control than had the Turco-Egyptians before them, with British support and expertise. Moreover, a Mahdist attempt to advance northwards into Egypt was defeated in August 1889 by the Egyptian army under General Francis Grenfell. Already fragmented by disputes over the succession to the Mahdi and weakened by famine and disease, the Khalifa's regime survived only a few years longer.

Darfur

Before going on to look at the end of the *mahdiya*, let us divert our attention westwards to Darfur. Even readers who know little about Sudan will probably have heard of Darfur. In 2003, ethnic cleansing of the people of Darfur became a *cause célèbre* in the USA and elsewhere for prominent campaigners like George Clooney. The term *janjaweed* - for the bands of armed riders who swept down on villages to kill the Fur, Masalit and Zhaghawa men and rape, kidnap or displace the women and children - became part of the international vocabulary. Antonov aircraft indiscriminately dropped makeshift barrel bombs. Helicopter gunships fired on the villages.

President Omar al-Bashir's regime in Khartoum responded robustly to international criticism of the use of the *janjaweed* as a proxy militia against the Darfur rebel groups. The violence that developed since 2004 is the latest phase in a series of conflicts over the past several decades. Their roots lie variously in political, economic and social marginalisation of Darfur, the ambitions and influence of Libya and Chad, Arab supremacism and Islamism. Despite numerous ceasefires and peace agreements and the presence of a joint African Union-United Nations peacekeeping mission, the conflict is by no means fully resolved today.

Darfur was always different from the rest of northern Sudan. The people of Darfur have tended to look west to Chad rather than east to the Nile valley. In modern times, the ethnic links with Chad have at times translated into support from Chad for the Darfur rebels, at times into Chad's cooperation with Khartoum.

We can probably date the birth of Darfur to the seventeenth century, when Suleiman Solon founded the Keira dynasty. The dynasty collapsed in the 1870s when the then Sultan, Ibrahim, challenged the slave-trader Al-Zubayr Rahma Mansur of Bahr el-Ghazal, the region to the south of Darfur. Al-Zubayr's mercenaries defeated the Fur fighters and killed Sultan Ibrahim. Darfur became part of the area under Turco-Egyptian control, but Britain was already wielding substantial influence. Under Gordon's governor-generalship of Sudan during the *turkiya*, Rudolf Freiherr von Slatin took over Darfur in 1881 as Governor.

In many ways, Rudolf von Slatin's story draws together the themes of the previous sections. He also represents an example of nineteenth-century European interconnection that two world wars almost erased from our modern memories.

Von Slatin was born in a village 10 km west of Vienna and, after studying at the *Handelsakademie* - the business school - in that city, he made his way to Cairo to work in a German bookstore. He did not stay long in Cairo, but set off in 1874 to explore Sudan, eventually meeting up with German-Jewish physician Dr Eduard Schnitzer ('Emin Pasha').

Schnitzer had qualified as a physician in Germany, but found medical employment in the Ottoman Empire. He worked in Equatoria in southern Sudan, not just as Chief Medical Officer but also as a naturalist and as Charles Gordon's emissary in Uganda. He later succeeded Gordon as Governor of Equatoria.

Rudolf von Slatin visited Equatoria and the Nuba Mountains during the 1874 journey, but did not meet Charles Gordon. Before returning to Austria to complete his obligatory military service, he asked Dr Schnitzer to recommend him to Gordon for employment. Four years later, he was serving in July 1878 as a lieutenant in Crown Prince Rudolph's Austrian regiment on the Bosnian frontier. One day, he was delighted to receive a letter from Gordon, now Governor-General of Sudan, inviting Slatin to work for him.

Rudolf von Slatin

Von Slatin arrived in Khartoum on the 15th January 1879. After he had spent a few months unsuccessfully trying to inspect the unscrupulous tax collectors, Gordon appointed him *mudir*, or governor, of the district of Dara in southwestern Darfur. He was to start at once, in order to conduct military operations against the son of a former Sultan, who was trying to regain control of Darfur. An Austrian working for an

Englishman who reported to an 'Egyptian Turk' of Albanian descent, Rudolf von Slatin was by then just twenty-two years old.

After several battles and skirmishes at the head of Turco-Egyptian troops, 'pacifying' rebellious tribes and slave-traders, this young man was appointed Governor of the whole of Darfur in April 1881. Here he eventually found himself trying to stem the tide of the Mahdist rebellion that was sweeping across Sudan. His troops were progressively losing their will to fight, rightly believing that the days of the Turkish occupation were numbered.

The danger of mutiny was ever present, and Slatin got wind of such a plot. By instructing his servant to hide and eavesdrop in a house where the ringleaders were meeting, he was able to confront them with evidence of their plans. The six men confessed, were brought before a court martial and sentenced to death. Slatin confirmed the sentence and the men were shot.

However, his rule was not seen as especially harsh. He privately asked a trusted Egyptian officer for his honest opinion of what the men thought of the punishment, of the fact that he had only punished the ringleaders, and of being led by a European. The answer was surprising. 'Although not accustomed to such severe discipline,' answered Mohammed Farag, 'they are fond of you, and you are beloved by the men because you pay them regularly ... This year we have had very heavy losses, and the men are getting tired of continual fighting.' But that was not the main reason. 'You wish me to tell you the truth,' said Farag,

> Then here it is: they do not object to you on account of your nationality, but on account of your faith. The idea has got about in the battalion that in this religious war you will never be able to gain a victory, and that in every battle you fight you will suffer great losses, till at length you yourself will be killed.[19]

The Mahdi's propaganda was powerful. For Slatin's men, the issue was not the relative strengths of the opposing forces. Rather, they believed that they could never win in battle if they were led by a Christian. Slatin's solution, driven by his sense of duty to the Khedive, was both pragmatic and dramatic. Next morning, he paraded the battalion and spoke the words before them that indicated his acceptance of Islam. He became a Muslim. When this action became known in Britain, Slatin's reputation paid a heavy price. But he achieved the immediate effect he desired. The men fought bravely under him and they won several local battles.

It was to no avail. The Mahdi's advance from his conquests in Kordofan was inexorable. Belief in his divinity spread. Hicks Pasha's force was annihilated at El Obeid. Recognising that he could not expect relief from Hicks, Slatin bowed to the inevitable and surrendered Darfur, although the people of the capital, El Fashir, continued to resist the Mahdi's troops for a few weeks more. Slatin himself was summoned to an audience with the Khalifa[20] and eventually with the Mahdi, to whom - for whatever reason - he publicly pledged allegiance. 'Adhere closely to the Khalifa and devote yourself entirely to his service', instructed the Mahdi.

Thus it was that Slatin, while secretly wishing for the Mahdists to be defeated, became a servant of the Khalifa and travelled with him and the Mahdi, effectively as their prisoner, on their trek to Omdurman and Khartoum to besiege Gordon's force (see previous section). But on the way Slatin came under suspicion. Armed men seized him. 'Two large iron rings, bound together by a thick iron bar, were slipped over my feet, and then hammered close,' he later wrote, 'an iron ring was placed round my neck, and to this was attached a long iron chain with the links so arranged that I had the greatest difficulty in moving my head'.

The Mahdi's forces took Omdurman and besieged Khartoum. Although the relief force under Sir Garnet Wolseley repelled attacks en route by the 'Dervishes', the Mahdi pre-empted its arrival and attacked Khartoum. The defenders scattered. Gordon's severed head was brought to the Mahdi in Omdurman and triumphantly shown to Rudolf von Slatin. The *mahdiya* was established.

Five days later, a group of soldiers deposited Slatin in the common prison, secured with an even heavier set of shackles. He remained a prisoner of the Mahdi, and subsequently a household slave of his successor the Khalifa, for twelve years. As well as humiliating the former ruler in public by making him walk barefoot, the Khalifa wished to keep a close eye on him and head off any possible military threat from the British in Egypt. Nevertheless, Slatin's family in Austria provided money and Reginald Wingate, Director of Intelligence in the Egyptian Army, paid friendly Arabs to provide camels for Slatin's escape across the desert. After several failed attempts, in 1895 Slatin made his escape and undertook the perilous journey to the Nile at Aswan. On reaching safety, he received telegrams of congratulations from Austrian diplomats in Cairo and Reginald Wingate in Suakin. He travelled by steamer to the southernmost railhead and arrived in Cairo a few hours later. Exhausted, Slatin spent a year recovering from his ordeals, but went on to join the Intelligence Branch of the Egyptian Army. He served under Herbert Kitchener in his campaign to reconquer Sudan. Queen Victoria knew and respected Slatin; she awarded him several honours, as did Emperor Franz Joseph I of Austria.

Britain in Egypt

Since 1889, Britain's settled policy had been to resist any interference by a European power that threatened her control of the Upper Nile. Britain had been in effective control of an economically weakened Egypt since 1882, to counter a nationalist threat and maintain access to the Suez Canal shipping route to the Far East. The Egyptian Army was organised under British officers; subordination to the Ottoman Sultan was only nominal.

Having repulsed the 1889 Mahdist invasion of Lower Egypt, Lord Salisbury's government did not see occupation of Sudan as a major priority. However, Salisbury saw an opportunity. He authorised an Egyptian invasion of Dongola in northern Sudan in March 1896. Italy had requested this, to divert the Mahdist threat to her position in Ethiopia. Brigadier Horatio Herbert Kitchener was by then the Commander-in-Chief - the *Sirdar* - of the Egyptian Army. He commanded the invading force.

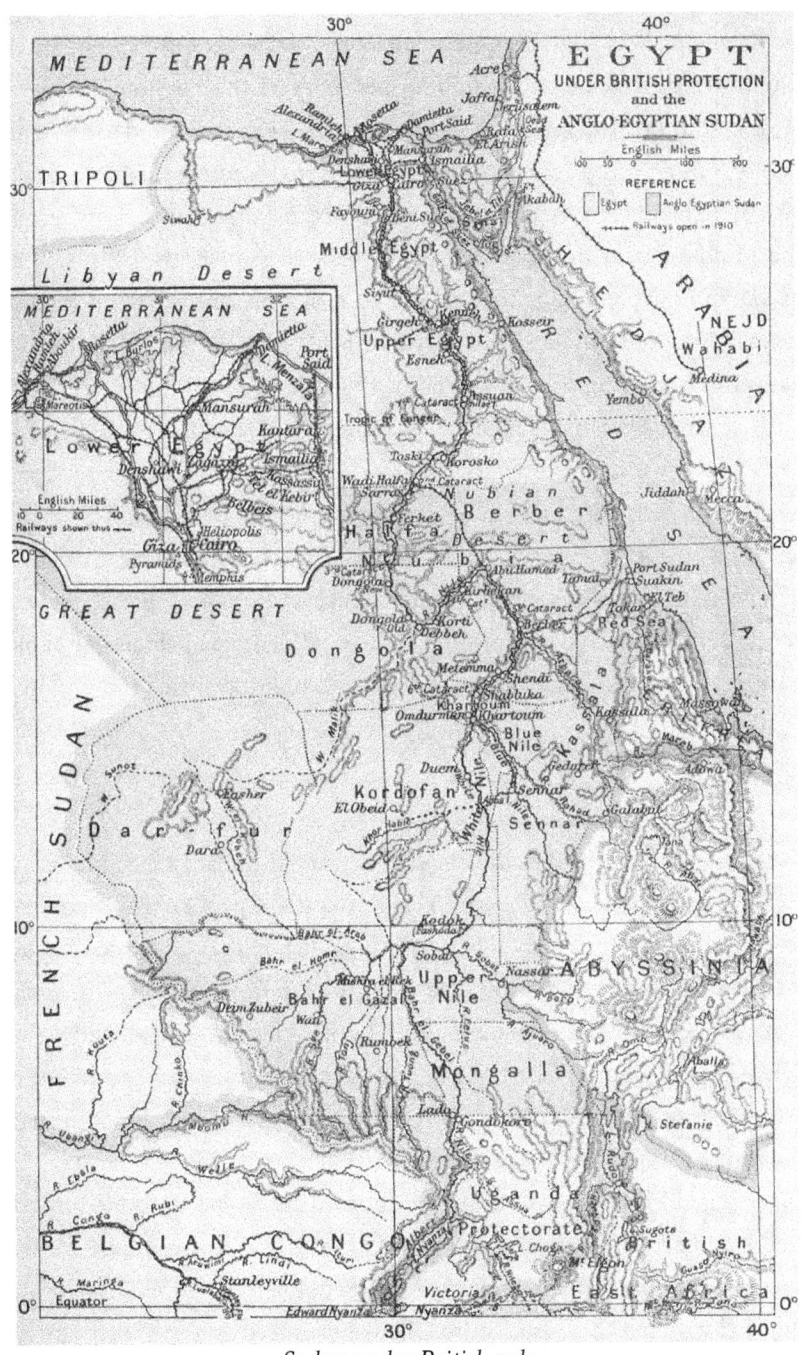

Sudan under British rule

Kitchener was an impressively tall, blond-haired, moustachioed Royal Engineers officer, better known to posterity as the face on the iconic World War I recruitment poster. He had been born in Ireland to an Army family, but grew up in Switzerland. As a Royal Engineers officer in the 1870s, he had taken part in surveys of Palestine and served elsewhere in the Middle East, gaining a high proficiency in Arabic. By 1898, he had served in Egypt and Sudan for fifteen years and had been *Sirdar* for six of them. Along the way, he had battled with the Mahdi's armies on various occasions, receiving a facial wound in 1888.

Kitchener's British-Egyptian invasion of Dongola in 1896 was supported by a newly built railway and by river gunboats. It took the Mahdists by surprise and succeeded with minimal British and Egyptian losses. The Egyptian army consolidated its occupation and instigated regular river patrols as far as Merowe. Back in London, the success was greeted with tentative optimism. A more confident and belligerent public attitude to the fearsome 'Dervishes' was starting to replace the previous caution.[21]

Kitchener and Omdurman

1898 was a crucial year in the colonial history of Sudan, a turning point. On 7th April of that year, over 11,000 British, Egyptian and Sudanese troops marched for twelve miles through the night. Their goal was a fortified encampment surrounded by a thorn fence - a *zeriba* - near the Atbara river, where *ansar* commander Emir Mahmud Ahmad had set up defensive positions. The smoke of scattered fires indicated the extent of the enemy camp. At dawn, an Egyptian artillery bombardment pounded the *zeriba*, followed by the steady advance of a broad line of infantry. The *ansar* fought bravely, but could not withstand the assault by trained troops well supplied with modern weapons. The battle was over by 8.30 am. Several thousand fighters under the command of Emir Osman Digna had slipped away, but thousands were killed or captured. Many of the captives were African slave soldiers who were more than willing to change sides.

The most prominent exception was the leader, Mahmud Ahmad.

The captured Emir Mahmud Ahmed with Kitchener, Atbara 1898

This 'tall, strong Arab, about thirty years old' was brought to Kitchener, who asked him 'Why have you come into my country to burn and kill?'. 'I have to obey my orders, and so have you', retorted the sullen but dignified Mahmud, who also warned that the slaughter at Atbara would be avenged at Omdurman. The conversation was reported by the young Winston Churchill, who was present at the battle in a dual capacity: as a subaltern in the 21st Lancers and as a correspondent for the Morning Post. How Churchill knew what Kitchener and Mahmud had said to each other in Arabic is unclear. If true, though, we might wonder what Kitchener meant by 'my country'.[22]

The Khalifa would have to wait several months to attempt vengeance at Omdurman, as the Anglo-Egyptian Army spent the hot summer in camp, resupplying and reinforcing their positions. Three new gunboats were ordered from Britain, shipped by sea and rail to northern Sudan and constructed on site. The Expeditionary Force comprised 8,200 British and 17,600 Egyptian soldiers, equipped with 80 artillery pieces and 44 of the new Maxim machine guns on land and river. More than 2,500 horses,

3,500 camels, and 1,000 mules and donkeys provided mobility. Preparations complete, on 27th August 1898 the Force started a slow, cautious advance southwards along the west bank of the Nile.

On 1st September, the cavalry moved forward to reconnoitre Omdurman, Winston Churchill leading a troop of the 21st Lancers. They spied a vast army of about 50,000 men, outnumbering their own by two to one, advancing towards the Egyptians and British. The Khalifa had decided that his best option was to attack. As evening approached, the Dervish army halted its advance. It became clear that they would not attack that day. The attack was expected at dawn.

Before dawn on 2nd September, Kitchener arrayed his troops a few miles north of Omdurman, in a long crescent defensive formation facing away from the Nile. River gunboats protected the flanks of the crescent. When the attack came, it was a direct frontal assault. Long before the Mahdi's followers came close enough to fire their own weapons with any effect, artillery decimated their advance. The courageous fighters pressed on in the face of the withering fire of the Maxim machine guns. This is the persistent image of the Battle of Omdurman.

The Khalifa's plan was much more ingenious than a simple frontal attack, involving forces held in reserve for flanking manoeuvres in response to the various possible contingencies. But it failed. The power of modern weapons, together with the crucial contribution of gunboats, allowed Kitchener to defeat the much larger Dervish force. Once the Khalifa's initial attack had collapsed, Kitchener ordered his force to advance. 'We've given them a good dusting,' he said after just five hours, as thousands of Mahdist fighters lay dead or wounded on the battlefield. The remnant fled as the Anglo-Egyptian army continued its march into Omdurman. Some individuals surrendered. Those who resisted were shot or bayoneted. Kitchener rode to the Mahdi's Tomb in the centre of Omdurman, released thirty prisoners and took possession of the town. The prisoners included German merchant Karl Neufeld, who had set out from Aswan on 1st April 1887 to Kordofan with a party of men and a female servant, to collect ostrich feathers and gum arabic. Betrayed by their guides, the party had been attacked by Mahdists under orders to capture Neufeld alive. They had massacred all but the female servant and Neufeld, who remained a virtual prisoner at Omdurman and Khartoum for twelve years, until freed by Kitchener.

The Khalifa, having failed to mount a substantial defence of Omdurman, fled. He reached El Obeid, but the Mahdists could never again challenge the power of the Anglo-Egyptian occupiers.

The British press saw Kitchener's victory as a fitting vengeance for Gordon's 'martyrdom', even though countering the challenge to colonial rule in Africa was more important to the Government. According to one of the more balanced reports, reflecting the colonialist thinking of the age,
> If Gordon is "avenged", it is in the only effective way, by the completion of his work. He desired to win these provinces for civilisation. They have been won. It is touching to read how the Sirdar honoured the hero's name on Sunday. He went to Khartoum, though Khartoum is but a ruin. He hoisted the British and Egyptian flags there over the Palace in which Gordon died. He held a service in Gordon's memory. It was a fitting, as well as a generous and a beautiful, tribute. But for Gordon, in all probability, no British army would now be there. His heroic adventure engraved the name of the place on the heart of the nation.[23]

Soon afterwards, Queen Victoria elevated Kitchener to the peerage as Baron Kitchener of Khartoum and of Aspall. In early 1899, he became Governor-General of Sudan and consolidated the Anglo-Egyptian grip on the country.

The Fashoda Incident

While Herbert Kitchener was occupying Dongola and progressively driving the Khalifa's forces back from Atbara and Omdurman, an international crisis was developing 3,000 miles away in Europe. Its focus was a small town in the Sudanese interior, whose name would become a watchword for European imperialist rivalry.

The town of Fashoda[24] on the White Nile was the traditional capital of the Shilluk kingdom. The political and religious leader of the Shilluk, the king or *reth*, lived in Fashoda. But, like the Iraqi Saddam Hussein's palaces in a later day, the hut where he would be sleeping on a given night was unknown. The sons of any former *reth* stood to succeed him when he died, so he was theoretically in danger from his sons, brothers and uncles. And the fear was not unjustified. If a *reth* showed signs of physical imperfection - like illness, sexual impotence as reported by one of his wives, or just old age - he was no longer considered fit to rule. Retirement was not an option. Regicide was in order. To protect the *reth*'s life, potential successors were generally raised in a distant village and forbidden to enter Fashoda at night.

Politicians in London knew none of this when they heard that Major Jean-Baptiste Marchand had entered and claimed Fashoda on 10th July 1898 on behalf of the French Republic, after a long march through the French Congo. But they recognised the significance of the French presence in an upstream area of the Nile. It placed a barrier between British interests in Egypt and East Africa. It threatened the flow of waters that formed the lifeblood of Egypt. Diplomacy had successfully neutralised German and Italian threats, but the danger posed by the French was a different matter. This required military intervention.

Twelve years earlier, German Chancellor Otto von Bismarck had convened a conference of the European powers in Berlin. Britain, France, Germany and Portugal negotiated their claims to African territory, carving up Africa between them. Competition continued, though, to gain control of areas of Africa not already claimed: the 'Scramble for Africa'. Britain already held sway over Egypt and much of East Africa. If France could gain control of an area between the two regions and of the flow of Nile waters to Egypt, British supremacy in the eastern part of Africa might be undermined.

Major Marchand was a French soldier and adventurer who had spent the early part of his military career exploring West and Central Africa. In January 1897, the Government in Paris sent him with a small party on a dangerous mission. His task was to raise the French flag in the Sudanese interior. Marchand, with a party of eight French officers and 120 soldiers recruited in Niger, had battled for nearly two years across Africa on his hazardous mission. British intelligence officers had heard something of the expedition, and there were inklings in the press that the French were at Fashoda. Belligerent statements in the Paris newspapers suggested that 'the tricolour of France will be found much more difficult to haul down than the standard of the prophet'.[25]

Locally, the first firm evidence came just a few days after the fall of Omdurman. One of the Khalifa's river boats returned from the White Nile on 7th September. The crew were surprised to find Omdurman in Anglo-Egyptian hands and quickly surrendered. They reported upon interrogation that, transporting a 500-man mission to collect grain, they had been fired upon at Fashoda by troops under white officers flying an unknown foreign flag. The foraging party had disembarked downstream of Fashoda, with two gunboats, and sent this unfortunate crew back to ask the Khalifa for reinforcements. Bullets dug out of the boat's hull proved to be of European origin.

Three days later, Kitchener took a substantial force in five steamers to investigate. They dealt speedily with the disembarked Dervish force and continued upstream to Fashoda. There Kitchener met Marchand, who congratulated him on his victory at Omdurman and welcomed him to Fashoda in the name of the French Republic. Kitchener had a far superior force at his back, while Marchand's situation was precarious; his small force was well equipped but perilously short of supplies and ammunition.

Nevertheless, Kitchener did not seek confrontation. He did not insist that the French tricolour be lowered but raised the Egyptian flag. Leaving a substantial garrison a few hundred yards from the French camp, he placed restrictions on Marchand's freedom of movement, pending a diplomatic solution between London and Paris. Some tensions arose when Marchand left his more chauvinistic deputy in charge while he travelled to Cairo to seek his government's instructions, but otherwise the two parties at Fashoda coexisted amicably. The French depended on the Anglo-Egyptian garrison for food.

Back in London, the 'Fashoda Incident' assumed a greater significance in British eyes than it perhaps warranted. The newly won victory at Omdurman was being snatched away. In diplomatic negotiations between London and Paris, the British approach was robust and the French eventually took a conciliatory line. On 5th November, Lord Salisbury announced that he had received a note from Paris: the French party at Fashoda would withdraw. Marchand returned to Fashoda and led his men away, with Anglo-Egyptian support and cordial farewells. The French donated their remaining champagne and wine to the British officers' mess. Only after the French had left was the British Union Jack hoisted alongside the Egyptian flag.

In Paris, attitudes were less positive. This was the cruellest humiliation since 1871, according to one newspaper. Marchand returned to Paris and became the idol of the French nation. For his bravery in crossing Africa and confronting the British, he was promoted to Commander of the *Légion d'honneur*.

Of course, nobody reflected very much on what the Shilluk people thought of it all.

The Legacy of the Nineteenth Century

Apart from the century when the 'Black Pharaohs' held sway over the whole of Egypt, much of the history we have so far seen shows a Sudan whose resources and people were plundered by more powerful foreigners.

In the nineteenth century, too, the country's rich, varied culture and heritage were subordinated to the goals and ambitions of outsiders. First it was Muhammad Ali, the Albanian merchant's son for whom Sudan was the ground to play out his ambitions for territorial expansion, to build a family dynasty to rival the Ottoman Empire. Later, Sudan became a battlefield for European imperial rivalry, against a background of an orientalist fascination with the Middle East. In both periods, the country was a source of wealth: of grain, of ivory, of slaves.

Between the two came a period of relative independence for Sudan. The *mahdiya*, riven as it was with division and religious strife, at least represented control of the central areas of Sudan by Sudanese. Yet for the South, to the extent that the Mahdists penetrated it at all, the period was no less colonial in nature than the *turkiya* before and the Anglo-Egyptian 'Condominium' that followed, to which we now turn.

CHAPTER FOUR

The Condominium

A Colony but not a Colony

What to call the administration of the newly conquered Sudan was a ticklish problem. It was not a British colony, because Egypt was part of the Ottoman Empire, even if under rather a loose grip. Yet Egyptian bankruptcy under Khedive Ismail had given Britain effective control over Egypt's finances. And Britain had invaded Egypt in 1882 to put down an Army-backed revolt and restore the Khedive's authority. By 1899, British officers controlled the Egyptian army and British officials were in strategic positions in the administration. Britain was effectively in control of Egypt, and would not easily give up her interests in the Nile waters and Suez.

It was Evelyn Baring, later 1st Earl of Cromer, who came up with the idea. Baring was a member of the famous London banking family who had made a name for himself as an administrator in colonial India and in Egypt. As Consul-General in Cairo alongside a weak Khedive, he wielded immense power. Lord Cromer proposed an artificial construct for shared sovereignty and governance of Sudan, combining Egyptian claims with British colonial interests. Sudan would be called a 'condominium': an area jointly 'owned' by Egypt and Britain. (The word is familiar to American readers in the context of jointly owned apartment buildings.)

The Khedive of Egypt would appoint a British Governor-General of Sudan but would be required to follow British advice about the appointment. Sudan would be a British colony in all but name.

Lord Cromer, 1901

The supposed partnership between Egypt and Britain had practical consequences. The Governor-General in Khartoum did not report to the

Colonial Office, which administered most British colonies around the world with a fairly firm hand. Instead, he was answerable, through Cromer in Cairo, to the Foreign Office in London. Sudan was not high on the list of priorities for the Foreign Office, so both Cromer and the Governors-General who reported to him had a great deal of autonomy. More importantly, any incentive to invest in Sudan was almost entirely absent.

So developed the sometimes-condescending rule of Sudan by men who were fascinated by the Middle East and Africa, and who devoted the greater part of their lives to the region. After Herbert Kitchener's short period as Governor-General, administering the territory his Anglo-Egyptian troops had conquered, he was replaced in 1899 by Sir Reginald Wingate.

Wingate had been born near Glasgow in 1861 but grew up in the Channel Islands. After joining the Royal Artillery, he spent most of his military career in the Arabic-speaking world. His competent grasp of the language gained him a role as Kitchener's Director of Military Intelligence during the Sudan campaign. He had stood alongside Kitchener at Fashoda during the famous meeting with Jean-Baptiste Marchand. And it was a force under Wingate's command that defeated the last remnant of the Khalifa's army. Reginald Wingate served as Governor-General until 1916, long enough to establish the tone of the administration. Its backbone was the Sudan Political Service.

The Sudan Political Service

The first administrators in the Condominium were seconded officers of the Egyptian Army, but this did not last. Lord Cromer saw the need for civilian administrators, not least because the military might be called away. Indeed, many were, to fight in the Boer War. He again came up with a creative solution: the Sudan Political Service. The SPS would provide what were eventually called District Commissioners in Sudan's regions. In the half-century of the SPS's existence, its members totalled fewer than 400. Probably little more than 100 were in service at any one time over the vast territory of northern Sudan.

What was needed, stated Cromer in the elitist language of the time, was a cadre of 'active young men, endowed with good health, high character, and fair abilities ... not the mediocre by-products of the race, but the flower of those who are turned out from our schools and colleges'.[26] The main places to look for these young men were the elite universities of Oxford and Cambridge. Specifically, the place to look was on the sports field.

The idea of 'first-class hearties with third-class minds' has been the prevailing stereotype of the SPS, and at least the first part holds some truth.[27] Almost one-third of SPS officers were Oxford or Cambridge 'Blues', having represented their university in sports such as cricket, boxing or rowing. Several had represented their country. Yet the stereotype is misleading; many were also academically gifted. A higher-than-average proportion had gained first class degrees, and many later proved themselves experts in a variety of fields. Indeed, their immersion in the culture of their allotted areas led to some of the most important accounts of Sudanese ethnology.

Much as for the British intelligence services, professors in the Oxford and Cambridge colleges were asked to look out for likely candidates. Harold MacMichael was one of those picked out. As an undergraduate in Cambridge, he visited the orientalist Professor E G Browne at Pembroke College to ask for help in interpreting a brass seal sent to him from Delhi. The professor talked to him about the East for an hour, and suggested he apply for Sudan. After facing a selection board headed by Sir Reginald Wingate, MacMichael returned to Magdalene College to study Arabic for a year. In 1905, he sailed for Sudan with six colleagues from Oxford and one from Trinity College, Dublin. MacMichael spent twenty-eight years in Sudan, rising to the most powerful position in the Khartoum administration under the Governor-General. Later, as High Commissioner of the British Mandate of Palestine from 1938 to 1944, Sir

Harold MacMichael survived seven assassination attempts by Jewish partisans.

The SPS men were carefully selected, received language training in Arabic and were then sent to manage alone in remote outposts of the country. It was a demanding task, involving responsibility and autonomy remarkably early in life. The men needed energy and initiative, working long hours in a hostile climate. The possibility of disease was never far away. In return, they were well paid, given extensive home leave for recuperation and promised retirement at the age of fifty.

One SPS man, Wilfred Thesiger, was already an experienced traveller when he became an assistant district commissioner in Darfur in 1935. He had grown up in Addis Ababa in a British diplomatic family and hankered after adventure. During his first summer vacation when reading history at Magdalen College, Oxford, after leaving Eton, 'he set off alone, working his passage on a tramp steamer to Istanbul and returning third-class by train'.[28]

For his second 'long vac', he tested his own endurance by spending a month on a Hull fishing trawler off Iceland. After Oxford, he explored 'Abyssinia's Awash River and the forbidding Aussa Sultanate with its Danakil nomads'.

Like many of his SPS colleagues, Thesiger had represented his university at sport. He had captained the university boxing team and had his nose broken by his Cambridge opponent.

He was in his element in Darfur, where he 'first learned to travel by fast-riding camel with local companions, dressing as they did, eating local food out of the same bowl, and asking nothing of technology but a good rifle, a torch and a compass'.

Whereas other members of the SPS used their leave to return to Britain, Thesiger sought further adventure. During one leave, he 'completed a long and dangerous journey to the almost unknown Tibesti mountains in the Sahara'. He loved the desert; he was 'exhilarated by the sense of space, the silence, and the crisp cleanness of the sand'.

Wilfred Thesiger 1934

During the war, Thesiger joined the Sudan Defence Force as a junior officer and won the Distinguished Service Order in 1941 for his courageous leadership in the fight against Italian forces. He later served in the fledgling Special Air Service in North Africa. In his later years, he became famous as a traveller in Africa, the Middle East and Asia, on foot, by camel, horse, mule or donkey.

A contemporary of Thesiger was Douglas Dodds-Parker, who had read modern history at Magdalen College, Oxford. Unlike Thesiger, his interest was in international politics. For his long periods of leave, he took a map of Europe and the Middle East and 'set out a different route to be followed each year'.[29] In 1933, it was Palestine, Syria, Iraq, Stalin's Russia and Hitler's Germany. In 1936, he visited the Balkans, Poland, the Baltic States and again Russia and Germany. In 1937, he travelled further afield, covering 14,000 miles in the USA and Canada. In Sudan, he spent three years in Kordofan, a similar period working directly for the Governor-General in Khartoum, and a further three years in Blue Nile Province close to the Ethiopian border. Here he developed a network of underground contacts in Ethiopia, by now occupied by Italy.

After the outbreak of the Second World War, Dodds-Parker joined Britain's Special Operations Executive, but he was soon back in Khartoum. As a member of SOE, he served under Colonel Orde Wingate organising subversion and sabotage in Ethiopia against the hated Italians. In 1941, he played a crucial role in the ejection of the Italians and the return of Emperor Haile Selassie to his native country.

For such a small number of men to administer the population in such a large area, an appropriate political system was needed. The British colonial system of indirect rule relied on traditional tribal structures that already existed. The elitist, class-ridden culture that pervaded the early Political Service is by today's standards, at best, anachronistic. Yet, as Robert Collins suggests, an innate moral sense of Christian duty among the British upper classes, together with the teamwork of the sportsman, translated to a feeling of responsibility and service in remote areas of Sudan. The young men administered their areas paternalistically, but in collaboration with the traditional leadership. Most devoted themselves to the Sudanese for many years. Whatever we may think of them being there at all, they have been widely recognised as being among the most effective of British colonial administrators.[30]

The Sultanate of Darfur was treated differently.[31] It had been incorporated in Sudan by the Mahdists, but was for part of the Anglo-Egyptian period not included in the Condominium. The hereditary Fur Sultan, Ali Dinar, had defeated the remaining Mahdists in El Fashir and reclaimed his territory. In 1900, Khartoum recognised his independence, which he maintained with brutality. Usefully for the Condominium, he fought off French incursions from Chad to the west. Sir Rudolf von Slatin, by now Inspector-General of Sudan, persuaded the Rizeigat tribal leaders to the south to surrender to Ali Dinar and accept his rule. In the 1914-18 war, however, the Sultan took the Turkish side. British troops defeated his followers in 1916, killed him and re-incorporated Darfur into Sudan. The British relied on indirect rule in Darfur as much as anywhere in Sudan, so that investment in infrastructure and education were minimal. The seeds of marginalisation were being sown.

As the SPS spread its administrative net across northern Sudan, Anglo-Egyptian troops suppressed any resurgent outbreaks of Mahdism. Slavery too was on its way out. Charles Gordon had asserted in 1879 that the slave trade was at an end. This rash claim was given more weight during the Condominium, but only gradually and with a great deal of tolerance for the long-standing Sudanese institution. According to Governor-General Kitchener's directive of 1899, 'Slavery is not recognised in the Sudan, but as long as service is willingly rendered by servants to masters it is unnecessary to interfere in the conditions between them'.[32] Slaves could request and immediately gain their freedom, but were then by no means out of the woods. Employment and accommodation were difficult to find. One member of the SPS did something about this: he set up villages for former slaves. They called themselves 'the sons of Arkell'.

Anthony Arkell joined the SPS in 1920 after serving in the Royal Flying Corps and Royal Air Force and being awarded a Military Cross. Apart from his concern for former slaves, his main interest was in archaeology and anthropology. He became commissioner for those fields in 1938, and led several excavations in Sudan, focusing particularly on Darfur. After his return to England in 1948, he became professor of Egyptology at University College London, and wrote an influential history of Sudan in 1955.

A later and somewhat less cerebral example of the versatility and energy of the SPS men was Ranald 'Ran' Laurie, father of the actor Hugh Laurie. Ran Laurie joined the SPS in 1936 and eventually became District Commissioner of Nyala in South Darfur. But he is best known as an oarsman. He learned to row at Monkton Combe School near Bath and continued his rowing career at Selwyn College, Cambridge. He was in the winning Cambridge boat for the Oxford-Cambridge Boat Race in 1934, 1935, and 1936. In the 1936 Berlin Olympics, he rowed for Great Britain, but his greatest triumph was a gold medal in the coxless pairs race in the

1948 Olympics at Henley-on-Thames. His rowing partner, Jack Wilson, was also one of his SPS comrades.

The pair's Sudan experience earned them the nickname 'The Desert Rats' among the Olympic commentators. Laurie later studied medicine and worked for thirty years as a general practitioner in Oxford. His actor son Hugh rowed for Cambridge in the 1980 Boat Race.

SPS men were encouraged to stay single, especially in the early days. Later some of them married, but only the bravest of British women were willing to take on the role of a District Commissioner's wife. A R Walmsley, in his Foreword to Rosemary Kenrick's account of the lives of these women, writes:

> The men of the Sudan Political Service, a dedicated band addicted to economy and impervious to discomfort, spent much of their lives on trek, and when they were at base they seemed to regard their rather primitive living-quarters as a superior form of tent.
>
> Husbands were therefore not the least of the obstacles facing their wives, who struggled to establish something resembling a home, in surroundings which lacked almost everything we take for granted, in searing heat or torrential rains, some hundreds of miles from help or from a neighbour.

One woman recalled:

> Once, while waiting for my husband to appear for lunch at 2.30, I glanced across at our water jug. A very large rat was standing on its hind legs, freely lapping.
> On B.'s return I said, "I'm afraid I can't stay married to anyone who has rats drinking his drinking water. I am leaving you". B. replied, "How actually will you leave?" Lacking a camel or any other practical transport to the railhead five hundred miles away, that put a stop to the conversation.

As Walmsley writes, this was 'a world which has now disappeared where, for fifty years, labouring in extreme conditions, a tiny foreign élite could run a vast country in preparation for its independence'.[33] While the negative aspects of colonial history are clear, the role of a small number of dedicated Britons in establishing northern Sudan's transport infrastructure, economy, education and health system is hard to deny.

The South

At first, the sort of men who took responsibility in southern Sudan differed greatly from those of the Sudan Political Service. Although navigable channels through the swampy Sudd to the savannah beyond had been discovered and opened up, travel was still a challenge. The dozens of independent tribal groups, dominated by the Dinka and Nuer, fought each other and resisted control by the British. The South was ruled, and progressively pacified, by military officers on contract, partly using locally recruited Equatorian troops. Their isolation and the harsh conditions led these 'bog barons' to act with independence, taking on the role of paternal autocrat and benevolent despot, ruling 'by the power of panache, personality, persuasion and prestige'. They did little to reduce the ethnic rivalry that persists in South Sudan today.

F D Kingdon recounts the story of a raid against the Nuer in 1927-28, with Royal Air Force bombers in support.[34] The account illustrates the difficulties encountered by the British in southern Sudan's hostile and unfamiliar environment and the danger of unintended consequences, including provoking hostile long-term reactions. This was the transition period, as civilians took over administration of southern districts from contract officers.

Nuer tribesmen, nursing a simmering grievance, had killed District Commissioner Vere 'Fergie' Fergusson on 14th December 1927. Fergusson had insisted on returning stolen cattle to their Dinka rivals. The British gradually assembled three columns of about 200 troops, each supported by a further 200 reluctant porters, servants, guides and interpreters, for a punitive patrol.

After completing planning on Christmas morning and eating Christmas dinner, the officers of the Rumbek column made final preparations and set off on 2nd January. They trekked through dried-up swamp and long grass, stopping well short of sunset each day to erect the protective barbed-wire fence that they were carrying with them. The

Nuer were known to be 'brave and crafty fighters', and an attack was always a danger.

At the third overnight encampment, Nuer 'crept up from every side with blood-curdling yells and [according to the interpreters] threats of what they were going to do to us'. Soon after dusk, a porter who had lagged behind the column rushed to safety inside the wire. The naked Nuer warriors, thinking this was a signal, attacked prematurely. Their spears were no match for rifles and machine guns. They fled, leaving behind them six of their dead, to be found next morning. Officers from one of the other two columns, camped nearby, came over and reported that they 'had caught a herd of cattle, and not being able to take it along they had to slaughter it ... with a machine gun'.

The arbitrary punishment of the 'offenders' continued. The British could not catch the Nuer, who were 'quite capable of keeping out of our way indefinitely ... they could always get news of our approach and withdraw into the swamp with their cattle. No one felt inclined to follow them up, nor did it appear to be any use'. Instead, the British 'had a quiet day burning the houses of the Nuer who had fled'. Kingdon, for one, found that the job 'went against the grain, as the cattle-houses were beautifully built and very neatly thatched with new grass'.

Attempts to contact the Nuer rebels and persuade them to hand over the murderers were unsuccessful. The commander sent a message to HQ, requesting air support from the RAF. Meanwhile, they set about clearing a landing ground. Ten days later, on 20th January 1928, an RAF advance party arrived and set up a radio. They suggested that pilots should be given a letter to hand to any Nuer who might find them after a forced landing, offering a large reward if the pilot was brought alive to safety. 'It might have been a good idea', noted Kingdon, 'if any of the Nuer had been able to read and if any of us had been able to write Nuer'.

In line with proposals by Sir Hugh Trenchard, the first Chief of the Air Staff, that aircraft were the ideal means of policing the British Empire, the concept was that bombing would persuade the Nuer to give themselves up. Bombing of the Nuer cattle camps started on 24th January. Most of the Nuer warriors dispersed into the swamps, but enough came into the rallying points for contact to be re-established. Eventually, 'both sides thought they had had enough'. The aircraft returned to Khartoum and the British columns took a few Nuer prisoners back to Rumbek. Kingdon concluded that an offensive patrol 'does nearly as much harm as good'.

Thus the 'Southern Policy' - treating northern and southern Sudan differently - was established early in the Condominium period. It was more or less a by-product of the situation the British took over and the way they dealt with it. In the South, Arab traders were excluded; the use of English rather than Arabic was taught and encouraged. The Khartoum administration encouraged Christian missionaries to proselytise and provide education.

Juba 1936

Separate treatment was perhaps inevitable. The progressively formalised policy of indirect rule was more easily implemented in the

North. Traditional structures of governance were more clearly identifiable there than in the South. Also, the growth of an educated, intellectual elite and associated Sudanese nationalism in the North, especially in and around Khartoum, raised British concerns about common cause with Egyptian nationalists; indirect rule encouraged traditional governance and reduced this threat. Such a concern was not an issue in the South. So it was that the *de facto* separate treatment of the South developed primarily through pragmatism and expediency rather than ideology.

Towards Independence

In contrast to the neglect and marginalisation of Darfur and southern Sudan, the Anglo-Egyptian authorities of the Condominium encouraged economic development in and close to the Nile valley. Communications networks stretched their tentacles to key areas of northern Sudan. It became possible to communicate by telegraph and to travel by rail to places as far away as the newly opened Port Sudan in the East. The Gezira Scheme, launched by the government and private entrepreneurs in 1911, took advantage of newly irrigated areas of the fertile region between the White and Blue Niles to make cotton the most important Sudanese export.

Khartoum was again the commercial hub of the country, but also became the centre of Sudanese political activity, closely associated with the growth of education and an urban elite developed by the British for government service. Increasingly after the Egyptian revolution of 1919, a nascent movement among intellectuals in northern Sudan for independence and 'unity of the Nile Valley' – in other words, union with Egypt – became more evident, despite British support for traditional authorities through indirect rule. Britain had accepted Egypt's independence, leaving no basis for the continued existence of the Condominium. Britain and the new Egyptian government could not agree how to go forward.

Meanwhile, anger increased among nationalists in Egypt and Sudan. Rumbling disaffection developed among Egyptian troops stationed in Sudan, while Sudanese civilians and military cadets mounted demonstrations. The issue came to a head on 19th November 1924 when a group of students shot the Governor-General of Sudan, Sir Lee Stack, on a Cairo street. He died the next day.

The British reaction was immediate and dramatic. All Egyptian officers, troops and other public employees were required to leave Sudan. In the following year, the Sudan Defence Force was formed, with British and Sudanese officers. The SDF developed into an effective force. According to a British officer writing later, the SDF relied on the ingrained qualities of the Sudanese soldiers - hardiness, endurance and self-sufficiency - not 'drained out of them by excessive drilling on the parade ground, nor pampered out of them by giving them unneeded clothing and equipment'.[35] The men considered it a prestigious honour to serve in this Force, doing so as intensely loyal 'irregulars'; they either lived in their family homes or in soldiers' villages made up of the grass houses with which they were familiar.

Although indirect rule continued in the rural areas, the sense of a Sudanese national identity - at least in the North - progressively grew. From the mid-1930s, increased access to higher education for urban northern Sudanese under Governor-General Sir George Symes led to tentative attempts to introduce representative structures, such as the Graduates' Congress. But it also led to increased division among Sudanese along sectarian lines represented by political parties. The formation of the *ansar*-based National Umma Party (NUP) in 1945, calling for Sudanese independence in opposition to calls by the National Union Party for union with Egypt, was a particular turning point.[36]

The final years of the Condominium, influenced by revolutionary politics in Egypt and sectarian division within Sudan, saw turbulent, rapid and chaotic Sudanisation of administrative structures. Southern Sudanese, more or less ignored in the increase of higher or even secondary education, could take little part in these processes. Khartoum prepared for greater participation by the Sudanese in their own governance through a Legislative Assembly. Southerners feared that their interests would be overshadowed by those of the dominant northerners. This led to the 1947 Juba Conference, at which southerners – albeit with little choice - accepted existing British plans for the unity of Sudan and agreed to be represented in the Legislative Assembly.[37] A further Juba conference in October 1954 agreed southern support for Sudanese independence from Egypt, but set the condition that the new country would be set up as a federation, with autonomy for southern Sudan. It too was effectively ignored, and an independent Sudan was hastily inaugurated on 1st January 1956.[38]

POSTSCRIPT

War and Peace

Sudanese independence and the first civil war

My aim in this short book is to dig out the deep roots of Sudan's civil wars in distant history, rather than to recount better-known recent events. Others have written thousands of words about the period since independence in 1956, the two civil wars and the secession of South Sudan. I will cover these aspects more briefly in this chapter.

As independence approached, British officials progressively left the country. Officials appointed by the new Khartoum government took up their positions. It was not a smooth transition.

Even before the country formally became independent, unrest erupted in the South. Southerners were reacting to their exclusion from the rapid Sudanisation of the administration, justified by the new government because few southerners were 'qualified' for the positions. On 18th August 1955, a company of the Southern Corps at Torit mutinied and massacred large numbers of northern officers and civilians. The people of South Sudan see this as the beginning of the long struggle that led to their own independence in 2011. It was effectively the start of Sudan's first civil war.

The reaction to this rebellion was repressive, especially after General Ibrahim Abboud seized power in a military coup d'état in November 1958. President Abboud's policy of Arabisation and Islamisation in the

South, 'only succeeded in resurrecting old memories of the Turco-Egyptian administration, the slave trade and the *mahdia*'.[39]

Harassment of Christians and eventually the expulsion in 1964 of Christian missionaries led many southern politicians and Christian leaders to leave the country for Uganda and Zaire. A nascent political opposition in exile coalesced in the form of the Sudan African National Union (SANU). In parallel, armed guerrilla groups formed. Loosely united under the name Anya-Nya, they raided Government garrisons in Equatoria and Bahr el-Ghazal. Northern concerns about the regime's failure to solve the 'Southern Problem' led indirectly to a student-led 'October Revolution' in 1964, the downfall of Abboud, increased political turbulence and riots by southerners in Khartoum. A Round Table Conference in March 1965, involving the Khartoum government and various southern opposition factions, ended inconclusively after ten days.[40]

Failure to reach a political settlement led to hardened attitudes in Khartoum. The Army was effectively given a free hand to crush the increasingly effective armed southern guerrillas. Southern politician and soldier Joseph Lagu gained support from Ethiopia and access to weapons and training from Israel. He was able to suppress internal dissent, unify the Anya-Nya guerrillas under his own command and subordinate the exiled political opposition to the military. The political wing was established as the Southern Sudan Liberation Movement (SSLM). This enabled the united southern rebels to negotiate with the Khartoum regime.[41]

The 1972 Agreement brings 'peace'

A military coup by Colonel Ja'afar Nimeiri in May 1969 did not improve the success of the Army against the reinvigorated Anya-Nya. In July 1971, Nimeiri authorised his new Minister of Southern Affairs, Abel Alier, to develop earlier informal contacts with the SSLM in London into negotiations. As details of a potential political settlement were fleshed out, the Army was secretly ordered to reduce the intensity of the offensive in the South against Anya-Nya. Formal negotiations, facilitated by the World Council of Churches and others, resulted in the signature in March 1972 of the Addis Ababa Agreement.[42] The first civil war came to an end.

The agreement set up a semi-autonomous Southern Region with a Regional Assembly, but reserved significant powers for Khartoum. The process of assimilating Anya-Nya fighters into the Army began. Abel Alier became Regional President in the South.[43] The Addis Ababa agreement also unlocked external investment and aid, including support for major development projects. Many were too ambitious, among them the controversial Jonglei Canal, which was to divert water around the Sudd swamps for irrigation. American military and economic cooperation was forthcoming, in view of Nimeiri's supportive attitude to US Cold War goals; Communists had attempted a coup in 1971.

While the outside world rushed to provide development aid, there was little external sympathy for southern political concerns. As Robert Collins suggests, the text of the Addis Ababa Agreement may have been historically significant, but it was not matched by the mutual trust between North and South needed for successful implementation.[44] Southern expectations were not met.

Despite attempts by Alier and Lagu to maintain calm, the guerrilla movement Anya-Nya 2 mounted a series of attacks, against the background of interrelated political turbulence and division in North and South. Lagu, by now one of Nimeiri's Vice-Presidents, was advocating further division of the South into three regions, probably to reduce Dinka influence.[45] Nimeiri compromised with and to an extent neutralised northern Islamist opposition through a process of 'National Reconciliation' starting in 1977. In 1983, he emasculated southern structures of governance, imposed strict *shari'a* law and abrogated the Addis Ababa Agreement.

Colonel John Garang now enters the picture. Garang was an

Anya-Nya fighter who had trained in Israel, studied in the USA and Tanzania, and spent eleven years in the Sudanese Army after the 1972 Agreement. He was sent in January 1983 to quell a southern mutiny at Bor, but instead encouraged the mutineers to defect with him. They joined forces with the disparate groups of guerrillas, to become the Sudan People's Liberation Movement/Army (SPLM/A), based in Ethiopia. Eleven years of at least relative peace gave way to a second civil war.[46]

The Second Civil War

Military pressure from the SPLA progressively increased throughout southern Sudan and some bordering northern areas, particularly the Nuba Mountains.[47] Despite internal disunity and opposition from several southern militias, the SPLA was able to extend the area of southern Sudan under its effective control. It struck heavy blows against the essentially defensive Sudanese Army. The SPLA was able in 1984 to force Chevron to abandon oil operations and the French to give up work on the Jonglei Canal, both significant and prestigious development projects for Khartoum.

As today, southerners were by no means united and often divided on tribal lines. Remnants of Anya-Nya 2 sided with the Government in 1984. The Khartoum regime became adept at nurturing southern division and arming tribal militias (*murahalin*) such as the Misseriya and Rizeigat Baqqara, rather than employing regular troops.

In Khartoum, economic inequality, famine, and his own irrationality and isolation brought increasing unpopularity for Nimeiri. Following his attempts to suppress the Muslim Brotherhood, popular protest led to his overthrow in 1985 by yet another military coup.[48] The Transitional Military Council pledged a rapid return to democracy. Elections did take place in April 1986 as promised, but the SPLM/A boycotted them because security issues prevented large areas of the country from voting.

A coalition government took over, with Sadiq al-Mahdi as Prime Minister. Sadiq was not only head of the National Umma Party; he was also Imam of the *ansar* religious order and great-grandson of Muhammad Ahmad, the self-proclaimed Mahdi who captured Khartoum in 1885. Sadiq met John Garang in July 1986 in Addis Ababa, but dialogue ceased when the SPLA shot down a Sudan Airways aircraft, provoking a violent Government reaction. The divided coalition made little progress in resolving the 'Southern Problem'.

Meanwhile, the SPLA was making further military progress, particularly after John Garang's strategy with respect to opposing militias changed in 1987 from defeating them to winning them over.[49] Atrocities from both sides abounded, to become the fuel of recrimination for decades to come. In March 1989, the UN negotiated with both parties to provide famine relief by a consortium of UN and non-governmental agencies in southern Sudan under Operation Lifeline Sudan (OLS), which continued for nearly two decades.[50]. Sadiq pursued further negotiations in 1989, but an unexpected Islamist coup led by Brigadier Omar al-Bashir on 30th June 1989 pre-empted any possible agreement.[51] The state security apparatus became very effective at controlling the administration and justice system, suppressing opposition and nurturing ideological loyalty in the armed forces.

Within the SPLA in the early 1990s, John Garang's dictatorial style was militarily effective but provoked opposition and division, predominantly along Nuer-Dinka tribal lines.[52] Breakaway groups allied themselves with Khartoum, while Garang's position became weaker once Mengistu Haile Mariam lost power in Ethiopia in 1991. Experts often talk about the 'ripeness' of a conflict for resolution, and this situation was gradually developing in Sudan.

Various behind-the-scenes efforts and several official but uncoordinated attempts at settling the civil war took place in the next few years.[53] Many were regional. Relations between Sudan and her immediate neighbours have fluctuated, as internal politics within Sudan and the adjoining states has changed. But the regional dimension has always been an important element of the North-South Sudanese conflict. Factors such as common cross-border ethnicity – its historical roots lying in the artificial borders drawn by colonial powers - and economic rivalry (including for Nile waters) have led to support by neighbouring countries for Sudanese rebel groups, and vice versa.

But from September 1993 the regional influence was more positive. The governments of Ethiopia, Eritrea, Kenya and Uganda launched a more coordinated peace process under the aegis of the Inter-governmental Authority on Development. IGAD was to become the primary focus for negotiation in what became known as the Naivasha Process.

Peace Process

The IGAD negotiations or 'Naivasha Process' formed the backbone of more than a decade of often stormy negotiations between the Government of Sudan and the SPLM/A.[54] In May 1994, the two parties received a draft Declaration of Principles that recommended a 'peaceful and just political solution' based on the unity of Sudan, self-determination for the South, the recognition of diversity and the need for a 'secular and democratic state'.[55] An 'IGAD Partners' Forum' grouping of states and IGAD members endorsed these principles, which became the basis of future negotiation. But Khartoum fought a rearguard diplomatic action to avoid endorsing them.

The IGAD mediation did not achieve much for the seven years to 2001-2. What changed? One key event was '9/11', the attacks on the World Trade Center and the Pentagon on 11th September 2001. Although the Sudanese were already secretly cooperating with the USA on counter-terrorism, Khartoum became especially concerned about the USA's attitude to any state that was not actively engaged in the 'war on terror'. The Sudanese regime quickly did so. But there were other factors: a relative military stalemate and a feeling of war-weariness;[56] better coordination of international support for the process through a 'Troika' of the USA, UK and Norway; resolution by John Garang of his differences with his southern Sudanese rivals; and Kenyan President Moi's appointment of Lieutenant-General Lazaro Sumbeiywo to be IGAD's chief mediator.[57]

The process settled into formal bilateral negotiations between the two main parties, mediated by Sumbeiywo and his IGAD colleagues. Many interlocking issues - divisions within the North and the South, the conflict in Darfur, low-intensity fighting in eastern Sudan, the need for reconciliation after centuries of hatred - were all recognised. Yet, although the talks covered a broad spectrum, they were driven mainly by the interests of the Government and the SPLM/A.

The Comprehensive Peace Agreement, signed on 9th January 2005, triggered millions of dollars of international aid to support a new Government of National Unity in Khartoum and a devolved Government of Southern Sudan. Much of the money disappeared with little trace of the expected peace dividend for ordinary Sudanese. UN peacekeepers, consultants and NGOs flocked to southern Sudan. The economy of Juba boomed, reminding those who had known it before of a Yukon gold rush town.

South Sudanese Independence Celebrations, 9th July 2011

After six-and-a-half years of the Pre-Interim and Interim Periods, it was no surprise that the new state of South Sudan was called into existence. It would perhaps have been impossible to 'make unity attractive' during the 78-month gap between signature of the CPA and South Sudan's independence. Few Sudanese, from South or North, were in a mood to do so. The first six months were especially crucial. The death of Dr John Garang in a helicopter crash, a matter of days after being sworn in as First Vice-President, set back the implementation process severely.

Again, though, there were other factors. Once the agreement had been signed, the regional IGAD states took a back seat in the implementation process. Tension between Khartoum and the international community over Darfur continued. Slow implementation of development and governance measures meant that there was little sign of a peace dividend. So the fissures rooted in the colonial, pre-colonial and ancient history of Sudan were recognised but neither the CPA nor the independence of South Sudan provided a solution to them.

The modern Republic of Sudan

Conclusion

As this short book has focused on individual stories set in their historical contexts, it inevitably contains large gaps that more comprehensive histories fill. Also inevitable, given my own background and perspective, is the focus on the relationship between the Sudanese and the British.

Given the role of Britain in Sudan's history, it is no surprise that many Sudanese see British imperialism as an underlying cause of their problems. Perhaps a few older Sudanese remember some aspects of the British presence with fondness. Either way, the British imprint is never far below the surface, whether in the English spoken in South Sudan or the Union Jack layout of Khartoum's streets.

It works both ways. We British are noted more for our nostalgia than for our forward-looking orientation. Gordon of Khartoum, Lord Kitchener, the young Winston Churchill at the Battle of Omdurman: their stories loom large in popular British history.

The legacy of a violent past gets in the way of finding solutions to violent conflict, whether in Northern Ireland, Palestine or Sudan. History is of course not the only source of division. Cultural and religious difference, economic inequality, the 'curse' of rich resources like oil and inequitable access to them, the availability of modern weapons, international politics, global warming: all these factors can contribute to making violent conflict intractable.

Yet each of these factors has profound roots in the past. I have tried to unearth some of these deeper roots in the case of Sudan and South Sudan and to note how they affect today's politics. The relationship with Egypt, for instance, goes back centuries and even millennia. For many of those centuries, Sudan has been an area to dominate and exploit, whether in the time of the pharaohs, the Ottoman 'Turks' or the British-dominated Condominium. Today's relationship with other neighbouring states has also been affected by history; the boundaries marked out by colonial masters cut across areas of ethnicity and culture, making it difficult to construct national identity. Rebels find support and safe haven on the other side of the border.

Within Sudan and South Sudan themselves, division has often been an easier option than unity. Identity has been based on tribal and ethnic criteria, encouraged by British 'indirect rule' or 'native administration' in the North and by 'divide and conquer' pacification in the South. Geography has also played its part. The relative affluence of areas close to the Nile and the difficulty of travel, across inhospitable desert and impenetrable swamps, have led to marginalisation of outlying areas. Religion and culture too had a role. The advance of Islam and the Arabic language have cut across ethnic identity, but their exclusion from the South was an element of British 'Southern Policy' and reinforced the different character of the South. From 1956, the newly independent regime increasingly widened this north-south divide by emphasising the Arab-Muslim character of the northerners who controlled it.

All in all, a good deal of what scientists call path dependence – the present situation results from past events - has led to the divided Sudan and South Sudan we see today. One thing leads to another.

As I write, South Sudan's leaders have struck yet another peace deal that is meant to lead to the formation of a unity government later in 2019. The rivalry in South Sudan between Dinka and Nuer goes back centuries and the current violence can be seen as a continuation of the ethnic or tribal conflict. The Pope and the Archbishop of Canterbury have brought the leaders together in Rome. But both sides are dragging their heels and it is unclear that a unified South Sudan will result. We have been here before, and the signs are not positive.

In the North, the military has ousted President Al-Bashir following months of protests. The Transitional Military Council promises to hand over to civilians, but those manning barricades in the Khartoum streets are showing their scepticism and paying a price for it. Meanwhile, the involvement of outsiders is a key factor. The support of external powers like Qatar, Saudi Arabia and Sudan's more immediate neighbours for the different elements of the security forces vying to fill the power vacuum makes a peaceful transition difficult at best. For centuries, the ebb and flow in power struggles between different political factions has made consensus difficult to achieve. Again, we have been here before, even if with different actors.

Yet if any of us outsiders, whose forebears have contributed to this situation, might claim to represent a superior civilisation, we should pause for a moment. Also as I write, my own country is as deeply divided as I can remember, over our membership of the European Union. And the USA is one of the most polarised countries in the world. We live in glass houses. Who are we to throw stones?

In my years engaging with Sudanese from all parts of today's two countries, I have known many who wish only to coexist peacefully with their neighbours. Often theirs is the voice that is not heard, drowned out by the high-volume noise of recrimination and accusation. Perhaps a better understanding of conflict's origins may help us outsiders to be more constructive in supporting those who wish to resolve it.

Chronology

Date	Event
c. 2,300 BC	Harkhuf's journeys
c. 750-650 BC	25th Dynasty in Egypt ('Black Pharaohs')
c.600 BC – AD 500	Kushite kingdoms in Nubia
c.AD 400 -1500	Christian kingdoms (Nobadia, Makuria and Alwah)
AD 1637	Formation of Darfur Sultanate
1820-1885	Turco-Egyptian rule in Sudan (*turkiya*)
March 1881	Muhammad Ahmad ibn 'Abdallah self-identifies as the Mahdi and leads rebellion against Turco-Egyptian rule
5 November 1883	William Hicks defeated at El Obeid
26 January 1885	Charles Gordon killed following siege of Khartoum, signifying final Mahdist victory
22 June 1885	Mahdi dies, succeeded by Khalifa Abdallahi
1 September 1898	Khalifa defeated at Battle of Omdurman by British-Egyptian-Sudanese forces under Kitchener
19 January 1899	Anglo-Egyptian Treaty on Condominium signed
1916	Darfur incorporated into Condominium
26 August 1936	Withdrawal of most British troops from Egypt but continuing British control over Sudan under Condominium
12-13 June 1947	Juba Conference ostensibly supports inclusion of Southern Sudan in a unified independent state
18 August 1955	Mutiny of Equatorian troops at Torit
1 January 1956	Independence of Republic of Sudan
17 November 1958	Military coup by Major General Ibrahim Abboud
22 October 1964	'October Revolution' leads to fall of Abboud
6 December 1964	'Black Sunday' Southern riots in Khartoum
16-25 March 1965	Round Table Conference in Khartoum on 'Southern Problem'

25 May 1969	Military coup by Colonel Ja'afar Nimeiri
27 March 1972	Ratification of Addis Adaba Agreement
5 June 1983	Republican Order No 1 effectively abrogates Addis Ababa Agreement and Second Civil War begins
6 April 1985	Coup ousts Nimeiri, Transitional Military Council formed
24 March 1986	Koka Dam Declaration on 'New Sudan'
15 May 1986	Sadiq al-Mahdi forms coalition
30 June 1989	National Islamic Front-inspired coup brings Omar al-Bashir to power
December 1989	Peace talks convened by Jimmy Carter do not lead to agreement
20 May 1994	IGAD draft Declaration of Principles presented to Government of Sudan (GoS) and SPLM/A
20 August 1998	US missile attack on pharmaceutical plant in Khartoum, allegedly preparing chemical weapons
December 2000	Bashir re-elected for five years in elections boycotted by main opposition parties
6 September 2001	President George W Bush names Senator John Danforth as US special envoy for Sudanese conflict
11 September 2001	Terrorist attacks on World Trade Center and Pentagon
19 January 2002	Nuba Mountains Ceasefire Agreement signed by GoS and SPLM/A
20 July 2002	GoS and SPLM/A sign Machakos Protocol
February 2003	SLM/A and JEM rebels take up arms against GoS
9 January 2005	GoS and SPLM/A sign CPA, starting 6-month Pre-Interim Period and 6-year Interim Period
30 July 2005	SPLM leader and First Vice-President of Sudan John Garang killed in air crash, leading to riots in Khartoum and Juba
9 July 2011	Republic of South Sudan formed after 98.83% of southern Sudanese vote for independence
December 2013	Outbreak of civil war in South Sudan
11 April 2019	Military coup ousts Omar al-Bashir in Sudan

Research Sources and Further Reading

For those who wish to delve deeper, the Society for the Study of the Sudans UK (www.sssuk.org) and, in the USA, the Sudans Studies Association (www.sudansstudies.org) are academic organisations that organise conferences, promote learning and publish resources for anyone with an interest in South Sudan and/or Sudan. The Sudanese Programme (www.sudaneseprogramme.org) also organises occasional conferences and seminars in Oxford, UK, often at St Antony's College. In addition, Durham University is a major repository for resources on Sudanese history (Sudan Archive, Archives & Special Collections, Durham University Library, Palace Green, Durham DH1 3RN. Email: pg.library@durham.ac.uk.).

To supplement the references cited in the Notes, the following brief sections give a few research sources and suggestions for further reading. Website links were working at the time of publication.

Chapter One: Then Affects Now

Substantial accounts of the historical antecedents of Sudanese conflicts are provided in *The root causes of Sudan's civil wars: peace or truce*, Douglas Hamilton Johnson, 2011, and *Southern Sudan: too many agreements dishonoured*, Abel Alier, 1992. Informed accounts of the various phases of Sudan and South Sudan's civil wars and peace processes can be downloaded from the International Crisis Group website at:

https://www.crisisgroup.org/africa/horn-africa/sudan

and
https://www.crisisgroup.org/africa/horn-africa/south-sudan)

Chapter Two: Egypt and Kush

Aspects of the ancient history of Sudan are in *Outline of the ancient history of the Sudan - Parts I-III*, George A. Reisner, 1918, *Outline of the ancient history of the Sudan - Part IV*, George A. Reisner, 1919. More specifically, Harkhuf's travels are described in *Harkhuf's Third Journey*, G. W. Murray, 1965, whereas trading with Egypt by the Kush kingdoms is described in *Outline of the ancient history of the Sudan - Part V*, Dows Dunham, 1947, pp 5-6.

Three websites that cover the history of the Kush people and its relations with ancient Egypt are:
- https://discoveringegypt.com/ancient-egyptian-kings-queens/egyptian-dynasties-late-period/;
- https://www.ancient-origins.net/news-ancient-places-africa/nubia-and-powerful-kingdom-kush-002257;
- https://www.thoughtco.com/what-was-the-kingdom-of-kush-43955.

Chapter Three: The Turks and the Mahdi

Theodor von Heuglin and James Augustus Grant provide evocative first-hand descriptions of travels in nineteenth-century Sudan (*Travels in the Sudan in the Sixties*, Theodor von Heuglin, 1941, *A Walk across Africa; or, domestic scenes from my Nile Journal*, James Augustus Grant, 1864, pp 366-373). Anthony Arkell wrote an account of the early history of the Darfur sultanate in *History of Darfur 1200-1700 AD*, A. J. Arkell, 1951.

Chapter Four: The Condominium

A deeper understanding of the last two centuries of Sudan's history can be found from the writings of experts like Robert Collins, Douglas

Johnson, Peter Holt and M.W. Daly (*A history of modern Sudan*, Robert Collins, 2008, *The root causes of Sudan's civil wars: peace or truce*, Douglas Hamilton Johnson, 2011, *A history of the Sudan: from the coming of Islam to the present day*, P. M. Holt and M.W. Daly. 2000). Collins also describes Sudanese ethnic, linguistic and cultural diversity. Also, the relevant chapters of Mark Urban's book on British military leaders give good overviews of the careers of Charles Gordon and Herbert Kitchener (*Generals: ten British commanders who shaped the world*, Mark Urban, 2005). Winston Churchill's account of his experiences with the 21st Lancers in the Egyptian-British conquest of the Sudan (*The river war: an historical account of the reconquest of the Soudan*, Winston Churchill and F. Rhodes, 1902) reveals some of the attitudes of those who fought. The Sudan Political Service is well described in *The Sudan Political Service: a portrait of the 'imperialists'*, Robert Collins, 1972.

Chapter Five: War and Peace

See note on sources for Chapter One above.

Acknowledgements

This book derived from my research for a PhD at the University of Cambridge, where Dr Philip Towle patiently supervised my efforts. He and several other generous individuals then read drafts of the book, gave me helpful comments and saved me from numerous errors. Among those who devoted their time to helping me in this way are Philip Johnston, Rosalind Meryon and Steven McCormack, each of whom brought different perspectives and constructive insights. Members of my immediate family have encouraged and supported me in the writing process, too: Gabriela, Matthew and especially my wife, Ingrid, whose sharp eye spotted many an error. I am grateful to all.

However, this book is dedicated to the people of Sudan and South Sudan. Over the many years of my involvement with the Sudanese - of the North, South, East and West – I have enjoyed generous hospitality and experienced tolerance for an ignorant outsider. I have learnt a great deal. Although many have shared their knowledge with me, I am especially grateful to Dr Ahmed Al-Shahi of St Antony's College, Oxford, who took trouble over my text and clarified many points from his extensive experience.

For most Sudanese and South Sudanese, there is probably little to learn in these pages. I hope they will be patient with my attempt to help others around the world discover more about the history of their beautiful homeland.

List of Images

Image/Source	Page
Map of Sudan 1994, Public Domain (PD), University of Texas Perry-Castañeda Library	Front
Map of South Sudan, CIA World Factbook	3
Verdant garden in Darfur, 2008, by the author	5
Harkhuf from tomb at Qubbet el-Hawa, Creative Commons (CC, see https://creativecommons.org/licenses/by-sa/2.0/) 2010, by Karen Green	10
Empress Theodora, Basilica of San Vitale, Ravenna, CC 2015 by Roger Culos	14
Ruins of Church of the Granite Columns, Old Dongola, CC 2007 by Lucio A	15
Muhammad Ali by Auguste Couder, 1840, Biblioteca Alexandrina, PD (faithful reproduction of an original painting)	20
Muhammad Ahmad bin 'Abdallah, PD	27
The Mahdi's last letter, PD, Sudan Notes and Records 24, 1941.	29
Death of General Gordon at Khartoum, by J.L.G. Ferris, c. 1895, PD	30
Rudolf Carl von Slatin, Vanity Fair 15 June 1899, by Leslie Ward ('Spy'), PD City College of New York collection	33
Sudan under British rule, PD, Cambridge Modern History Atlas 1912	37
The captured Emir Mahmud Ahmed brought to Kitchener after the Battle of Atbara 1898, PD, National Army Museum	39
Lord Cromer, Vanity Fair 1901, by Leslie Ward ('Spy'), PD	48
Wilfred Thesiger, 1934, PD, from The Danakil Diary	52
Juba Hotel 1936, PD, Eric & Edith Matson Photograph Collection, Library of Congress.	58
South Sudanese Independence Celebrations 9th July 2011, CC 2011, Al Jazeera	69
Map: The modern Republic of Sudan, CIA World Factbook	70

About the Author

Dr Peter Dixon is a researcher, lecturer and author who writes nonfiction, with a focus on war and peace. He served for over 30 years as a Royal Air Force pilot and spent the next decade leading the charity Concordis International in its conflict resolution work in Sudan and other divided societies. He completed a PhD at the University of Cambridge in 2015 on intervention in civil wars. His writing has included *Amazon Task Force*, the story of a medical expedition in the Peruvian Amazon, *Guardians of Churchill's Secret Army*, which tells the stories of the men who joined the Special Operations Executive to keep Churchill's secret saboteurs safe, *Peacemakers: A Christian View of War and Peace*, and chapters in *Making Peace with Faith: The Challenges of Religion and Peacebuilding* (editors Michelle Garred and Mohammed Abu-Nimer) and *Locally Led Peacebuilding: Global Case Studies* (editors Stacey L. Connaughton and Jessica Berns). He and his wife Ingrid, also an author, work from their home in Gloucestershire, England, when their five grandchildren allow them to do so.

For more information, visit **https://cloudshillpress.com,**
where you can also join our email list and receive a free sample (ebook) chapter
of
Guardians of Churchill's Secret Army: Men of the Intelligence Corps in the Special Operations Executive

Bibliography

Akol, Lam. 2005. "Operation Lifeline Sudan", in *Accord 16: Choosing to engage: Armed groups and peace processes*, edited by Robert Ricigliano. London: Conciliation Resources.

Alier, Abel. 1992. *Southern Sudan: too many agreements dishonoured*. Oxford: Ithaca.

Anderson, G. Norman. 1996. interviewed by J. P. Moffatt: Foreign Affairs Oral History Collection, Association for Diplomatic Studies & Training (ADST).

Arkell, A J. 1951. "History of Darfur 1200-1700 AD." *Sudan Notes and Records* XXXII (1):37-70.

Asher, Michael. 2003. Obituary: Sir Wilfred Thesiger. *The Guardian*. Accessed 30 December 2018.

Boustead, Sir Hugh. 1971. *The wind of morning: the autobiography of Hugh Boustead*. London: Chatto & Windus.

Burckhardt, John Lewis. 1819. *Travels in Nubia*. London: John Murray.

Carney, Ambassador Timothy M. 2007. Some Assembly Required: Sudan's Comprehensive Peace Agreement. Washington DC: United States Institute of Peace (USIP).

Carney, Timothy M. 2006. interviewed by Sam Westgate: USIP and ADST Sudan Experience Program.

Churchill, Winston, and F. Rhodes. 1902. *The river war: an historical account of the reconquest of the Soudan*. Longmans, Green.

Collins, Robert. 1972. "The Sudan Political Service: a portrait of the 'imperialists'." *African Affairs* 71 (284):293-303.

Collins, Robert O. 2008. *A history of modern Sudan*. Cambridge; New York: Cambridge University Press.

Conflict Research Society. 1973. Intermediary Activity and the Southern Sudanese Conflict. London: Conflict Research Society.

Danforth, Revd John C. 2006. interviewed by W. Haven North: USIP and ADST Sudan Experience Program.

Davies, Reginald. 1957. *The Camel's Back: service in the rural Sudan*.

Dodds-Parker, Douglas. 1983. *Setting Europe Ablaze : some account of ungentlemanly warfare*. Windlesham, Surrey: Springwood Books.

Dunham, Dows. 1947. 'Outline of the ancient history of the Sudan - Part V.' *Sudan Notes and Records* XXVIII (1):1-10.

El Mahdi, Abdel Rahman, 1941, 'Correspondence: My father's last letter', *Sudan Notes and Records* XXIV: 229.

English, George Bethune, 1823. *A narrative of the expedition to Dongola and Sennaar under the command of His Excellence Ismael Pasha, undertaken by order of His Highness Mehemmed Ali Pasha, viceroy of Egypt.* Boston: Wells and Lilly.

Gilbert, Frederick E. 1997. interviewed by W Haven North: Foreign Affairs Oral History Collection, ADST.

God, Oil and Country: Changing the Logic of War in Sudan - Africa Report 37. 2002. International Crisis Group.

Gordon, Charles George. 1927. "Unpublished letters." *Sudan Notes and Records* X (1):1-59.

Gordon, Charles George, and Rosalind Meryon. 2012. *General Gordon on Golgotha: letters to the Royal Household from Jerusalem in 1883: General Charles Gordon of Khartoum to Sir John Cowell, Comptroller to the Household of Queen Victoria.* Jerusalem: The Garden Tomb.

Grant, James Augustus. 1864. *A Walk across Africa; or, domestic scenes from my Nile Journal.* Edinburgh; London: William Blackwood & Sons.

Griffiths, Aaron, Mark Simmons, and Peter Dixon, eds. 2006. *Accord 18: Peace by piece: addressing Sudan's conflicts.* London: Conciliation Resources.

Gulla, Sheikh Ali, 1925. The Defeat of Hicks Pasha. *Sudan Notes and Records* VIII: 119-123.

Hawley, Sir Donald. 2007. interviewed by Malcolm McBain. Cambridge: Churchill Archives Centre, British Diplomatic Oral History Programme (DOHP).

Holt, P. M. and M.W. Daly. 2000. *A history of the Sudan: from the coming of Islam to the present day.* London: Longman.

Idris, Amir H. 2001. *Sudan's civil war: slavery, race, and formational identities.* Lewiston: Edwin Mellen Press.

IGAD Declaration of Principles. 1994.

Jendia, Catherine. 2002. *The Sudanese civil conflict, 1969-1985.* New York: Peter Lang.

Johnson, Douglas Hamilton. 2011. *The root causes of Sudan's civil wars: peace or truce.* Kampala: Fountain.

Kenrick, Rosemary. 1987. *Sudan tales: recollections of some Sudan political service wives, 1926-56.* Cambridge: Oleander.

Kingdon, F. D. 1945. "The Western Nuer Patrol 1927-28." *Sudan Notes and Records* XXVI (1):171-178.

Kirk-Greene, A. H. M. 1982. "The Sudan Political Service: A Profile in the Sociology of Imperialism." *The International Journal of African Historical Studies* 15 (1):21-48.

Kontos, Ambassador C. William. 1992. interviewed by Thomas Stern: Foreign Affairs Oral History Collection, ADST.

MacMichael, H. A. 1956. *Sudan political service 1899-1956.* Oxford: Oxonian Press.

Murray, G. W. 1965. "Harkhuf's Third Journey." *The Geographical Journal* 131 (1):72-75.

Niblock, Timothy. 1987. *Class and power in Sudan: the dynamics of Sudanese politics, 1898-1985.* Basingstoke: Macmillan.

O'Neill, Joseph P. 1998. interviewed by Thomas Dunnigan: Foreign Affairs Oral History Collection, ADST.

Parsons, Sir Richard. 2005. interviewed by Malcolm McBain: Churchill Archives Centre, DOHP.

Petterson, Ambassador Donald. 1996. interviewed by Charles Stuart Kennedy and

Lambert Heyniger: Foreign Affairs Oral History Collection, ADST.
Pollock, John. 1993. *Gordon: the man behind the legend.* London: Constable.
Reisner, George A. 1918. "Outline of the ancient history of the Sudan - Parts I-III." *Sudan Notes and Records* 1 (1):3-15,57-79,217-237.
Reisner, George A. 1919. "Outline of the ancient history of the Sudan - Part IV." *Sudan Notes and Records* 2 (1):35-67.
Secretary-General, UN. 2001. Prevention of armed conflict. New York: UN Security Council.
Slatin, Rudolf Carl Freiherr von, and F. R. Wingate. 1896. *Fire and sword in the Sudan: a personal narrative of fighting and serving the Dervishes, 1879-1895.* Leipzig: Bernhard Tauchnitz.
Smock, David R., ed. 1993. *Making war and waging peace: foreign intervention in Africa.* Washington DC: USIP Press.
Sumbeiywo, Lt Gen Lazaro. 2006. interviewed by author.
Urban, Mark. 2005. *Generals: ten British commanders who shaped the world.* London: Faber and Faber.
von Heuglin, Theodor. 1941. "Travels in the Sudan in the Sixties." *Sudan Notes and Records* XXIV (1).
Welsby, D A. 1983. "Recent work at Soba East." *Azania: Archaeological Research in Africa* 18 (1).
Whitehead, G O. 1928. "Authors of Southern Sudan." *Sudan Notes and Records* XI (1):83-101.
Zartman, I. William. 1989. *Ripe for resolution: conflict and intervention in Africa.* New York: Oxford University Press.

Index

A

Abboud, General Ibrahim	63-64
Addis Ababa Agreement 1972	65
al-Bashir, Omar	31, 67
Ali Pasha, Muhammad	19-20
Alier, Abel	64-65
al-Mahdi, Sadiq	67
al-Taaishi, Abdullah (*khalifa*)	31, 35-36, 39-41, 43, 49
Alwah (or Alodia)	14-18
ansar (followers of the Mahdi)	28, 30, 38, 60, 67
Anya-Nya	64-66
Anya-Nya 2	65-66
Arkell, Anthony	54

B

Bahr el-Ghazal	26, 32, 64
Baker, Sir Samuel	25, 27
Baring, Evelyn, 1st Earl of Cromer	47-50
Beja	6, 17
Berlin Conference 1884-5	42, 54
Bog barons (contract military officers in S Sudan)	56
Burckhardt, Johann Ludwig (a.k.a. John Lewis)	22, 24
Byzantine Empire	14-15

C

Churchill, Winston	4, 39-40, 71
Cities and Towns	
Al-Fashir	17
Cairo	20, 26-27, 32, 36, 44, 47, 49, 60
Dongola	15-16, 36, 38
El Obeid	35, 41
Juba	1, 3, 58, 61
Kerma	12
Khartoum	5, 7, 22-33, 41, 48, 50, 52-53, 58-59, 61-72
Omdurman	5, 35, 38-41, 43-44, 71
Rome	72
Suba	16
Comprehensive Peace Agreement (CPA)	2, 4, 69, 70
Condominium (period of Anglo-Egyptian rule)	47
Countries	
Britain	4, 7, 25, 27-28, 30-32, 35-44, 47-48, 50-61, 63, 71-72
Chad	31-32, 53
Egypt	4, 6, 8-9, 11-17, 19-28, 31-32, 34, 36, 38-49, 53-54, 59-60, 64, 71
France	4, 19, 23, 42-44, 53, 66
Libya	31
Turkey	21
USA	11, 21, 31, 47, 52, 65-68, 73

D

Darfur 5-6, 17, 23-24, 31-35, 51, 53-54, 59, 69, 70
Dervishes (Western term for Mahdi's followers)   28, 35, 38, 40, 43
Dinka   6, 18, 56, 65, 67, 72
Dodds-Parker, Sir Douglas   52-53

E

Egyptian Kings (Pharaohs)
   'Black Pharaohs'   13, 44
   Amenhotep I   12
   Merenre   9-11
   Pepy II   11
   Thutmose I   12
   Tutankhamun   12
English, George Bethune   21
Equatoria   25, 32-33, 64

F

Fashoda Incident   24, 41-44, 49
Fergusson, Vere ('Fergie')   56
Funj Sultanate   16-18, 22

G

Garang, Colonel John   66-67, 69-70
gezira   5
Gladstone, William (British Prime Minister)   28-30
Gordon, Charles George ('of Khartoum') 25-30, 32-33, 35, 41, 54, 71

H

Harkhuf (Egyptian traveller)   9-11
Hicks, Lieutenant-General William ('Hicks Pasha')   28, 35

I

Inter-governmental Authority on Development (IGAD)   68-70
Islam 6, 14-18, 21, 24, 27-28, 31-32, 35, 66, 72

J

Jeremiah (Biblical prophet)   13

K

Khedive (Egypt)   21, 25-27, 34, 47, 48
Kingdon, F D   56
Kitchener, Brigadier Horatio Herbert   36, 38-43, 49, 54, 71
Kush (also Cush)   9, 12-14, 18

L

Lagu, Joseph   64-65
Laurie, Ranald ('Ran')   54

M

MacMichael, Sir Harold   50
mahdiya (period of Mahdist rule)   26, 31, 35, 45
Mahmud Ahmad, Emir   38
Marchand, Major Jean-Baptiste   42-44, 49
Muhammad Ahmad bin 'Abdallah ('The Mahdi')   27

N

Naivasha Agreement, *see* CPA

Nile River 1, 2, 4-6, 10, 13, 16-17, 22-23, 25-26, 32, 36, 40, 42-43, 47, 52, 59, 68, 72
Nimeiri, Colonel Ja'afar 64-66
Nobadia 14-16, 18
Nuba 4-6, 23, 33, 66
Nubia 9, 11-13, 15, 17-19
Nuer 6, 18, 56-57, 67, 72

O

Ottoman Empire 4, 17, 20-22, 28, 32, 36, 44, 47, 71

R

Riek Machar 3

S

Salva Kiir 3
Schnitzer, Dr Eduard ('Emin Pasha') 32-33
Shilluk 17-18, 42, 44
Slatin, Rudolf Freiherr von 32-35, 53
Slavery 6, 11-12, 16, 18-19, 22-26, 28, 32, 34-35, 39, 45, 54, 64
South Sudan, Republic of 1, 3, 4, 11, 18, 24, 56, 63, 68-72
Southern Policy 58, 72
Stack, Sir Lee 60
Sudan Defence Force 52, 60
Sudan People's Liberation Movement/Army (SPLM/A) 2, 7, 66-69
Sudan Political Service 49-51, 54-56
Sudd 4, 5, 18, 24, 56, 65
sufi (mystical form of Islam) 27, 31
Sumbeiywo, Lieutenant-General Lazaro 69
Symes, Sir George 60

T

Theodora, Empress (Byzantium) 14
Thesiger, Sir Wilfred 51-52
turkiya (period of 'Turkish' rule) 22, 32, 45

V

Victoria, Queen 25, 29, 36, 41

W

Wingate, Sir Reginald 36, 49-50, 53

Notes

1 *A history of modern Sudan*, Robert O. Collins, 2008, p 1.
2 *The river war: an historical account of the reconquest of the Soudan*, Winston Churchill and F. Rhodes, 1902, p 4.
3 *Sudan's civil war: slavery, race, and formational identities*, Amir H. Idris, 2001.
4 *Harkhuf's Third Journey*, G. W. Murray, 1965.
5 *Outline of the ancient history of the Sudan - Parts I-III*, George A. Reisner, 1918, p 225.
6 *Ibid*, p 234.
7 Jeremiah 38:6-13
8 In the early debate about whether Jesus was divine, human or both, the Monophysites asserted that his nature was only divine.
9 Quoted in *Recent work at Soba East*, D A Welsby, 1983.
10 *A narrative of the expedition to Dongola and Sennaar*, George Bethune English, 1823.
11 *Travels in Nubia*, John Lewis Burckhardt, 1819, p.70
12 Wilhelm Junker, quoted in *Authors of Southern Sudan*, G O Whitehead, 1928, p 94.
13 *Travels in Nubia*, John Lewis Burckhardt, 1819, p 324.
14 Quotes from *Unpublished letters*, Charles George Gordon, 1927.
15 *General Gordon on Golgotha*, Charles George Gordon and Rosalind Meryon, 2012; *Gordon: the man behind the legend*, John Pollock, 1993.
16 *Chinese Gordon for the Soudan*, 1884.
17 *Correspondence: My father's last letter*, Abdel Rahman El Mahdi, 1941.
18 *The Defeat of Hicks Pasha*, Sheikh Ali Gulla, 1925.
19 This and quotations in the subsequent paragraphs are from *Fire and sword in the Sudan: a personal narrative of fighting and serving the Dervishes, 1879-1895*, Rudolf Carl Freiherr von Slatin and F. R. Wingate, 1896.
20 The leader who was later to take over upon the Mahdi's death.
21 Churchill and Rhodes, 1902, pp 138-161.
22 *Ibid*, p 160.
23 London Daily News, 6 September 1898.
24 Today's Kodok in Western Nile State in South Sudan, about 70 km northeast of Malakal.
25 Echo de Paris, quoted in Aberdeen Journal, 2 September 1898.
26 Lord Cromer, Political and Literary Essays, quoted in *Sudan political service 1899-1956*, H. A. MacMichael, 1956, pp 1-2.

27 *The Sudan Political Service: A Profile in the Sociology of Imperialism*, A. H. M. Kirk-Greene, 1982, p 45.
28 This and the following quotes on Thesiger are from *Obituary: Sir Wilfred Thesiger*, Michael Asher, 2003.
29 *Setting Europe Ablaze: some account of ungentlemanly warfare*, Douglas Dodds-Parker, 1983.
30 *The Sudan Political Service: a portrait of the 'imperialists'*, Robert Collins, 1972.
31 See, for instance Collins, 2008, pp 275-277.
32 *The Camel's Back: service in the rural Sudan*, Reginald Davies, 1957, p 2.
33 Here and above *Sudan tales: recollections of some Sudan political service wives, 1926-56*, Rosemary Kenrick, 1987.
34 This and the following quotes about the patrol are from *The Western Nuer Patrol 1927-28*, F. D. Kingdon, 1945.
35 *The wind of morning: the autobiography of Hugh Boustead*, Sir Hugh Boustead, 1971, p 78.
36 Collins, 2008, pp 46-68; Sir Donald Hawley, 2007.
37 Abel Alier, 1992, pp 20-21.
38 Sir Richard Parsons, 2005, Abel Alier, 1992, pp 24-33.
39 Abel Alier, 1992, p 25.
40 Abel Alier, 1992, pp 27-32; Collins, 2008, pp 83-84.
41 *Class and power in Sudan: the dynamics of Sudanese politics, 1898-1985*, Timothy Niblock, 1987, pp 272-3.
42 Accounts of mediation of the first civil war, and early attempts to mediate the second, are in *Making war and waging peace: foreign intervention in Africa*, David R. Smock, 1993, pp 79-160; *Intermediary Activity and the Southern Sudanese Conflict*, Conflict Research Society.
43 *The Addis Ababa Agreement on the Problem of South Sudan*, 1972;*The Sudanese civil conflict, 1969-1985*, Catherine Jendia, 2002; *Southern Sudan: too many agreements dishonoured*, Abel Alier, 1992, pp 54-74.
44 Collins, 2008, p 112.
45 Ambassador C. William Kontos, 1992; Abel Alier, 1992, pp 204-208.
46 *The root causes of Sudan's civil wars: peace or truce*, Douglas Hamilton Johnson, 2011, pp 61-62; Alier, 1992, pp 256-272.
47 Frederick E. Gilbert, 1997.
48 Ambassador C. William Kontos, 1992; *A history of modern Sudan*, Robert O. Collins, 2008, pp 150-156.
49 G. Norman Anderson, 1996; Johnson, 2011, pp 83-87.
50 *Prevention of armed conflict*, UN Secretary-General, 2001; *Operation Lifeline Sudan*, Lam Akol, 2005, Frederick E. Gilbert, 1997.
51 Joseph P. O'Neill, 1998; *A history of modern Sudan*, Robert O. Collins, 2008, p 170.
52 Ambassador Donald Petterson, 1996.
53 Comprehensive accounts of the Sudanese conflicts and efforts at peacemaking may be found in *God, Oil and Country: Changing the Logic of War in Sudan - Africa Report 37*, 2002; Robert O. Collins, 2008; Johnson, 2011, *Accord 18: Peace by piece: addressing Sudan's conflicts*, Aaron Griffiths, Mark Simmons, and Peter Dixon, 2006.

54 For a helpful summary of the process, based on the Sudan Experience Project, see *Some Assembly Required: Sudan's Comprehensive Peace Agreement*, Ambassador Timothy M. Carney, 2007.
55 *IGAD Declaration of Principles*, 1994.
56 Professor William Zartman has written on 'hurting stalemate' and ripeness for conflict resolution. See *Ripe for resolution: conflict and intervention in Africa*, I. William Zartman, 1989.
57 Lt Gen Lazaro Sumbeiywo, 2006; Revd John C. Danforth, 2006; Timothy M. Carney, 2006.

www.ingramcontent.com/pod-product-compliance
Lightning Source LLC
Chambersburg PA
CBHW050440010526
44118CB00013B/1613